Lauren,

Wishing you great
success!

Jayne Latz
8/8/18

# COMMUNICATE UP THE CORPORATE LADDER

## How to Succeed in Business with Clarity and Confidence

## JAYNE LATZ, MA,CCC-SLP

INDIE BOOKS
INTERNATIONAL

ISBN-10: 1-941870-53-8
ISBN-13: 978-1-941870-53-2
Library of Congress Control Number: 2016934259

Designed by Joni McPherson, www.mcphersongraphics.com

INDIE BOOKS INTERNATIONAL, LLC
2424 VISTA WAY, SUITE 316
OCEANSIDE, CA 92054
www.indiebooksintl.com

For inquiries or requests, contact:
Corporate Speech Solutions, LLC
150 East 61st St.
New York, NY 10065
info@corporatespeechsolutions.com
www.corporatespeechsolutions.com

# CONTENTS

# ACKNOWLEDGEMENTS

This book could not have been written without the help and support of several people. It is one thing to have an idea and quite another to take that idea and create a product. Many years ago I decided to take my experience as a speech-language pathologist and transition into the business world. I had no idea at the time where I was heading on this journey. I did not realize how many people could benefit from my skills, knowledge, and expertise. Being a corporate speech-language pathologist shares one very important trait with a traditional speech-language pathologist: helping people. The difference in the corporate arena is that you are helping healthy, successful people to climb the ladder of success. Over the past ten years I have seen our training make a significant difference in the lives of our clients.

Shortly after I started my company, Corporate Speech Solutions, LLC, a team was formed; a team of highly trained, insightful, and creative speech-language pathologists. Together we built a company that offers resources to business professionals around the globe. Every member of my team, Paul Michaels, Alina Kaplan, Robyn Kitto, and Kathleen Edwards, has contributed to this book just by doing all that they have done over the past ten years:

providing the best training they possibly could. Thank you.

Special thanks must be made to Stacey Rimikis, who has been my creative partner for over five years. She is always able to understand my shorthand communication and translate it into what needs to be done. I could never have created this book without her.

Henry DeVries was patiently by my side (virtually) as I created this content-rich book. My goal was to take you, the reader, on a journey, and Henry guided me in the right direction. His patience was appreciated as I took many a detour until I arrived just where I wanted to be.

Last, a special thank you to you, the reader. Without you, there wouldn't be a reason to write this book. While reading this book I hope you will stop to practice and implement the suggestions. My wish for you is to practice the tools and techniques provided in these pages and to achieve great success in your personal and professional life.

# SECTION I

## Why Make the Climb?

# CHAPTER 1

# Are You Stuck on the Corporate Ladder?

You are highly talented, well-educated, and successful; however, you are just not moving up in your career as you had hoped.

If you are lucky, you have your annual review. Perhaps you are told your communication skills are holding you back. Almost daily I receive a telephone call where I am told of the employees who cannot be promoted or are not moving up the ladder because of their communication skills. For those who have been lucky enough to receive the feedback, you know what to do. Find the right training that will make the difference so you can continue the corporate rise. If you have not been lucky enough to be told you need to improve your communication skills, let this book be your motivation to take action.

My friend Jennifer is a bright young woman in the field of finance. She has a tendency, like many young professionals, to speak in vocal mannerisms that are common with young girls in college. She frequently presents with upspeak, which is the tendency to end sentences with an upward inflection, characteristic of one asking a question. Additionally, she uses many filler words, such as "like" and "you know," which can often be distracting to the listener. She did not seem to be aware of these speech habits until finally, one day this year, her boss suggested that she seek the help of a speech professional. She said she knew just the person.

Here is how to recognize the signs that your communication skills may be holding you back:

- Are people frequently asking you to repeat what you just said?

- Are people asking you to speak up because they have difficulty hearing you?

- Are you seeing looks of confusion on your listeners' faces?

- Are promotions passing you by?

If you answered yes to any of these questions, consider how often this is happening. If it is happening at least once a day, you don't need to wait for a trusted colleague or manager to advise you. You need to take action now.

Your situation is not unusual. There are many like you. The good news is that there are great resources for you. The time is now to begin the work to improve your communication skills. If you don't, it will be very difficult to move up the ladder.

Here are a few recent stories that show the impact of this training on one's professional success. These are all true stories based on actual clients of Corporate Speech Solutions, but the names have been changed in order to maintain the anonymity of our clients.

Irina, one of our non-native English-speaking clients, was working with one of my trainers to improve her clarity and confidence. During one of her sessions, Irina informed the trainer that her company asked her to do a presentation at the White House. Yes, *the* White House on Pennsylvania Avenue in Washington, DC where the President of the United States lives. Since overall confidence was a concern, we worked together as a team to prepare her for this momentous event. There were more than twenty presentations that day, and Irina was informed that hers was among the best presentations of the day.

Bill and Antoine, two senior executives from the same national consulting firm, contacted our company. They did not know each other, and they were located in different states, but in two months they would be facing an important interview with a panel of partners from around the country at a meeting to be held in Chicago. This meeting would determine whether or not they would become partners in their firm. Each of them had attended the same meeting the previous year and for different reasons did not get the promotion. Bill needed to work on his body language and his verbal delivery, and Antoine needed additional work on reducing anxiety while forming answers to challenging questions on the spot. Our team worked with them individually (Antoine in person and Bill via Skype) and prepared them for this important meeting. Thanks to their determination, they both received the promotion.

Judith, an articulate attorney who lacked confidence in her presentation skills, came to us at a turning point in her career. She was nominated to be a New York City judge but had to testify about her qualifications before a panel of fifteen judges. Through our training to improve her non-verbal communication skills, plus helping her to craft the right answers under pressure and deliver them in a confident and concise manner, she received the judicial appointment.

These are just a few of our hundreds of stories of clients who have successfully advanced their careers. This book is designed to give you the tools to succeed in your career by building clarity and confidence.

If you're reading this book, you most likely recognize that strong communication skills are essential to a successful career.

Several years ago I wrote an article for an online magazine. It provided information and techniques designed to improve business communication skills in the workplace. In the article, I referred to a technique (included in this book) designed to help reduce one's rate of speech. This article resurfaces from time to time. The only way I know that it is recycled is because when it does, I receive an e-mail—usually one, maybe two—requesting help in reducing one's rate of speech.  Last week, the very first week of the new year, the article apparently was published online. I immediately received over one hundred e-mails in twenty-four hours. I share this because the message is clear: strong communication skills are directly related to your business success and more and more professionals are recognizing that fact. Learning to speak clearly and to communicate your thoughts and ideas in a confident, concise, and masterful manner is one of the most essential elements of professional achievement. However, as simplistic as it may seem, communicating effectively in a professional environment is a skill that is developed over time.

In this book I will break down the many factors that contribute to strong communication in the workplace and guide you through how to use each aspect to your advantage. You'll learn strategies for a variety of skills, from improving the quality of your speech itself to using communication to navigate tricky professional situations. Along the way you'll find helpful tips and exercises for practice in order to build confidence in your business communication skills.

# CHAPTER 2

# The Quest for Clarity and Confidence

The four steps of communicating up the corporate ladder will help you achieve success. The first step will address the importance of proper breathing to develop a dynamic speaking voice. Learning to properly project your voice will create immediate changes in the way people respond to what is being said. Step one will also address the importance of clarity and will provide insights and examples into how to improve your pronunciation skills.

The second step addresses the important topic of confidence. People present with reduced confidence for a number of reasons. Our goal is that, by providing tips and techniques on better communication, you will naturally develop greater confidence. Having said that, step two reveals how our body language can convey confidence through our posture, eye contact, and even our handshake. This nonverbal communication can convey confidence even when you are not feeling confident. Last, in step two, we address aspects of our speech that convey a lack of confidence. These include varying intonation patterns such as the rising tone at the end of a statement or the distracting little filler words such as "um" and "uh."

Step three brings you into the corporate arena. To move up the ladder we have to communicate effectively in meetings and networking events. I have noticed that many individuals are not comfortable with starting conversations with strangers or even colleagues at meetings or events. Step three will address these concerns and more. This step on the ladder will also provide insight into crafting and leaving the perfect voicemail. This is often the first impression of you that someone will have, so you want to be sure to make it a good one. Tricky professional situations will also be addressed in this step. These situations include handling conflict and gossip in the workplace as well as possible miscommunication.

The final step addresses the prize—the promotion or new job. This step will share information to help you ace the interview, from building rapport to getting you ready for the big day. By going up each step you will address each and every aspect of communication that will help you to make a positive impression from the moment you enter a room.

There are three people who shaped or helped shape me into the person I am today: my mother, my father, and my husband. I was a shy girl and did not speak until I was three years old. Family friends worried about me, but my mother never did. She said, "Jayne will speak when she is ready," and I did.

One day, when I was a teenager, my mother came home from work and excitedly said, "I met the most interesting woman at work today. She is a speech-language pathologist." In those days, the early '70s, this was not a well-known career. I had never heard of it. My mother had never heard of it either. In fact, most people were not familiar with the field of speech-language pathology.

My father had always told my sister and me to become teachers—a very traditional role for females during a time when traditional roles were popular. But that day, when my mother told me about this career, I was immediately interested. In my mind, it was a position similar to a teacher (which would please my father), but with an area of specialization.

By the time I went to college, I was one of the few college freshmen that was laser-focused and knew exactly which path to pursue. I completed college and went on to get my master's degree at The George Washington University. For the next twenty years I worked in the medical field helping stroke patients and the elderly to recover their voices.

My father was an inspiration because he was an entrepreneur. He owned a retail furniture store and served as a role model for being my own boss. There was always something in the back of my mind telling me to create my own business. One year, while attending a professional conference for the American Speech Language and Hearing Association (ASHA) I met a group of colleagues who were involved in a small niche in our field called Corporate Speech-Language Pathology. The group was called Corspan; The Corporate Speech Pathology Network. A light bulb went off at that moment. I was so excited. This was the perfect path for me to pursue—the blending of my background as a speech-language pathologist combined with working in the business world. The goal would be to provide training to business professionals who would benefit from speaking with greater clarity and confidence while climbing up the corporate ladder.

When I returned home from the conference I began the mental design of my new company, while still working in my traditional position in the medical environment. My husband and I began to brainstorm on the name and eventually the logo for this new venture. My husband was, and still remains, a very important part of this journey. He is a physician who ran a large medical practice for more than twenty-five years. He knew what was needed to not just create a new business, but to ensure its survival. I refer to him as my trusted advisor and always value his input.

Corporate Speech Solutions, LLC was born in 2006 and since that time our company has helped hundreds of corporate professionals and small business owners overcome communication issues that were holding back their careers. It is my goal to share with you the knowledge I have acquired in the past ten years in order to help you rise up the corporate ladder.

# SUCCESS

# SECTION II

## The Four Steps

# CHAPTER 3

# The First Step: Speaking with Clarity

The way you speak is one of the most important ways to convey an air of confidence and success. Your tone of voice, rate of speech, and other non-verbal cues often say more about your message than your words themselves, and subtle changes in your voice and presentation can create a significant difference in how your message is received. The speed at which you talk, the intonation you use, and how loudly you speak all contribute to the way others are perceiving your message. This section will guide you through ways by which you can modify each of these aspects to maximize the confidence and professionalism you project through your speech.

## Vocal Care

Although it's vital to develop clear, confident speech habits for effective professional communication, all of that is pointless if your voice is not up to par. Your voice is the delivery system for your message. If your voice is strained, unpleasant, or not projecting effectively, it can distract from your message and make your speech difficult to understand. Keeping your voice strong and healthy takes work, but is essential to good speaking skills. Keep the following rules in mind to maintain a strong, clear voice that will deliver your message with greater impact.

**Stay Hydrated:** Drink plenty of water. One of the most important tips for a healthy voice is to stay hydrated. When the vocal cords are too dry, they don't vibrate properly and can negatively impact the quality of your voice. The simplest way to avoid dehydration is to drink plenty of water on a day-to-day basis, especially on days you will be giving a presentation or speaking to a group. Don't begin drinking water fifteen minutes before a presentation; begin hours before. In situations in which you'll be speaking for long periods of time, always keep a bottle of water on hand and sip it periodically. Also, be aware of other factors that can dry out your voice. Caffeine and alcohol are both dehydrating substances; if possible, limit your consumption of both prior to speaking in public. Some medications, such as antihistamines, can also have a drying effect. If you are taking such medications, be sure to counteract this effect by drinking more water than usual.

**Rest Up:** Speaking and projecting your voice involve a variety of muscles. Just like any other muscles, they can wear out more easily when you are tired. When the muscles involved in speech are fatigued, you will often notice that your quality of voice suffers. Try to get a good night's sleep, particularly when you know you will need your voice in top form the following day.

**Relax:** Tension in the muscles of the neck and throat can inhibit the vocal cords from working properly and, if not taken care of, cause problems such as nodes and polyps on the vocal cords. Stand in front of a mirror and try to project your voice; you may notice visible tension in the neck and throat. Before any speaking event, take some time for some simple stress reduction exercises, such as head, neck, and shoulder rolls.

**Eliminate harmful habits:** Each time you cough or clear your throat, your vocal cords slam against one another. Many people develop a nervous habit of audibly clearing their throat when speaking. This repeated trauma to the vocal cords can cause injuries and damage over time, which may require surgery and vocal therapy from a speech-language pathologist. If you find that you clear your throat regularly, try to eliminate this habit as soon as possible. You may wish to have a close friend or colleague let you know when you're clearing your throat so that you become more aware of the behavior. Once you've noticed when you clear your throat, try to figure out *why* you're doing it. Is it a nervous habit used to buy time? A safer and healthier strategy is to replace throat clearing with a simple pause or deep breath; not only is it healthier for your vocal cords, it will be less distracting to your listener. If you find that you're clearing your throat because it genuinely feels irritated, replace throat clearing with another behavior, such as a hard swallow or taking a sip of water, both of which can sooth irritation. Finally, if you experience throat irritation often, make an appointment with your doctor. Throat irritation can be a symptom of laryngopharyngeal reflux (LPR), a condition in which stomach acid enters the throat area. Over time LPR can cause serious damage to the vocal structures.

## Proper Breathing

Your breath is the power behind your voice. We often don't put a lot of thought into breathing, seeing it as something that happens naturally and doesn't require thought or practice. In order for your voice to be projected, it must be sufficiently supported. If you aren't breathing properly and getting enough air, you will strain your voice trying to be heard. Often people try to compensate for poor breath support by using muscular tension to increase volume. Over time, this will cause your vocal quality to suffer, and may cause physical damage to your vocal cords such as nodules and polyps, masses of tissue that form on the vocal cords due to vocal misuse or abuse. These prevent the vocal cords from closing properly, resulting in a hoarse or breathy voice. In addition to preventing damage, proper breathing will improve your volume, pacing, and aid in relaxation as it provides you with more oxygen. So how exactly does one go about breathing properly?

First, take a deep breath and concentrate on your body's behavior. Does your chest rise as you breathe in? If so, you aren't breathing as efficiently as you should. As you inhale, your lungs should expand downward; when this happens, you should feel your lower-ribcage and stomach expand outward. This expansion is what allows you to take a deep, full breath and allows you to speak without tension in your throat. If you have trouble mastering this technique, lie on your back with your hand on your stomach and take a deep, relaxing breath as though you were about to go to sleep. When in this position, our body naturally reverts to proper breathing. After you've gotten used to how this type of breathing feels, stand up and take a few deep breaths, maintaining the technique. Then, practice speaking aloud with this type of deep breathing.

Once you have mastered proper breath support, you should be able to speak for longer periods of time without taking a breath. A good technique for increasing your breath support is to read aloud from a book. Start by reading a short sentence. Read this sentence repeatedly, adding a few words to the end each time. Using your deep breathing technique, see how many words you can read in one breath. Over time, using proper breathing, you should be able to increase the length of time you're able to speak in one breath. Use the following exercises to help you get started. Read each successive line, increasing the amount of speech you are able to produce on one deep breath:

- When is the meeting?

  When is the meeting that Dave organized?

  When is the meeting that Dave organized to discuss the proposal?

  When is the meeting that Dave organized to discuss the proposal that Sarah wrote?

  When is the meeting that Dave organized to discuss the proposal that Sarah wrote about the new client?

  When is the meeting that Dave organized to discuss the proposal that Sarah wrote about the new client in Afghanistan?

- Where were you?

  Where were you last Thursday night?

Where were you last Thursday night at eight o'clock?

Where were you last Thursday night at eight o'clock when I tried to call you?

Where were you last Thursday night at eight o'clock when I tried to call you about the presentation?

Where were you last Thursday night at eight o'clock when I tried to call you about the presentation that you were supposed to prepare?

Where were you last Thursday night at eight o'clock when I tried to call you about the presentation that you were supposed to prepare for today?

- Where is the archived file?

Where is the archived file that I need?

Where is the archived file that I need to help me with my project?

Where is the archived file that I need to help me with my project on statistical analysis?

Where is the archived file that I need to help me with my project on statistical analysis which is due tomorrow morning?

Where is the archived file that I need to help me with my project on statistical analysis which is due tomorrow morning before the meeting?

Where is the archived file that I need to help me with my project on statistical analysis which is due tomorrow morning before the meeting with the accounting department?

## Rate of Speech

One key aspect of speech that can be modified to project confidence, clarity, and professionalism is how quickly you speak. There is a variety of information conveyed in your rate of speech, including how confident you are in your message. Learning to strategically control your rate of delivery will project confidence, clarity, and professionalism.

Many people, when nervous or excited, tend to speak too quickly. Rushing through your words not only makes it difficult for others to understand you but also makes it seem as though you are nervous and trying to get speaking over with as quickly as possible. Be aware of this pitfall and concentrate on using a controlled, even rate of speech. This will help you to appear confident and knowledgeable about the topic on which you're speaking and will give your listener the impression that what you have to say has value and is worth taking the time to listen to. It also creates a sense that you are calm and in control. When speaking at an easy, relaxed rate, others have the time to absorb each point of your message as you speak, which increases the impact of your message.

While you want to avoid rushing your words, it's also important to make sure that your rate of speech doesn't slow to the point of dragging. Speech that is overly slow and plodding can cause you to lose your listener's attention. For maximum communication and confidence, find the middle ground between a rushed rate of speech and one that is sluggish and dull. The best way to do this is to pay attention to your listeners' reactions as you speak. Take note of their facial expressions and body language to get a measure of how your message is being received. Is your audience glancing at phones or other electronic devices? Do they look confused or overwhelmed? Are they frequently asking you to repeat what you said? You may need to slow down a bit. Do they appear bored, disinterested, or irritable? You may be speaking too slowly.

If you still feel that finding a moderate, appropriate rate of speech is a challenge, there are other more direct ways of obtaining feedback. One method is to choose a short passage and make a video of yourself reading it aloud at several different paces. Then watch the recording with a friend or colleague who is able to provide honest feedback and ask the person for his or her opinion on the given rates. Once you have found one that is comfortable, clear, and confident, practice speaking aloud and reading at that pace, using the given recording for reference. With practice and patience, you can achieve the perfect rate of speech for projecting confidence and professionalism while holding the full attention of your listeners.

**Pausing**

One powerful tool for regulating your rate of speech is the pause. When we're speaking quickly, we often neglect to pause and thus allow our speech to come out in a flood of words. This causes the speaker to lose much of the vocal variety that makes speech powerful and interesting to the listener. Inserting a well-timed pause can help to restore a natural flow and subsequent dynamic energy that will give more power to your speech and immediately engage your audience.

However, it's not enough to just pause; you want to make sure you're pausing in the most powerful places possible. Usually this is either right before or right after an important point to which you want to draw your listener's attention. Pausing before an important point allows the listener to fully focus and builds anticipation. Pausing immediately after you make an important point allows your listener to absorb the information and react to it. When properly used, silence can be worth a thousand words.

How long a pause you should take will depend on the circumstances. For example, you might pause briefly between sentences, but may take a longer, more obvious pause when shifting topics or emphasizing an important point. Pausing occasionally while speaking will not only help you to slow down, but will give your audience a chance to fully process the information. Taking the time to pause will also help you to control your breath support. Each time you take a significant pause, take a deep breath. As discussed in the previous section, maintaining strong breath support while speaking will help you to maintain a steady powerful volume and tone, helping you to come across as clear and confident. Mastering the power of the pause will have a tremendous impact on the delivery of your message.

## Strategic Marking System (SMS)

A great example of when to pause begins with your personal and professional introduction. Instead of saying, "Hello my name is JayneLatz," as so many often do, say, "My name is Jayne // Latz". This is of crucial importance to those individuals who have more than two syllables in both their first and last names. If there is no pause, there's a risk of the listener misunderstanding your name. In today's global marketplace, there are few names that are common to all listeners. By pausing between the first and last names, your listener will have a greater chance of understanding at least your first name. The same goes for the introduction of your company: "My name is Jayne / Latz. /// I am President of / Corporate / Speech Solutions." ///

Now let's practice with a typical business conversation. Try reading the following passages aloud, using the marks below as a guide for how and when to pause.

/ = short pause, used to emphasize a particular word or point

// = mid-length pause, used to break up sections of a sentence or add particularly strong emphasis to a word or phrase

/// = long pause, generally used between sentences

1. Sir? // I'm sorry to bother you. /// May I come in? /// As you know, / I've been with the company for thirteen years now. /// I feel that I'm an excellent worker: // I come to work on time every day, / my work is of the highest quality / and always completed on time. ///

However, / in all my years with the company, // I have never received a raise. /// I do love working here, // but frankly I can't survive on my current salary. /// I have two children now, // and unless you give me a raise, // I'll be forced to quit.

2. First of all, / I'd like to thank everyone for coming to this meeting on such short notice. /// I know you all have very busy schedules, // and taking time to meet up like this is not easy. /// However, / I think you'll be happy that you came today. /// As you are aware, / we have had a very good year: // sales have been higher than ever before, / and they show no signs of slowing. /// As a company, / we value our employees, // the people who make our success possible. /// As such, we'd like to make sure our appreciation is known. /// This year, / due to our success, / each of you will be receiving a $2,000 bonus / and two extra days of vacation.

## Volume

Nothing conveys confidence quite like a strong voice. Projecting your voice makes you sound authoritative and like a natural leader.

While you don't want to shout, speaking with a strong volume gives others the impression that you are saying something worth listening to. Speaking too quietly can make it seem as though you're not fully sure of what it is you're saying, or that you don't feel it's really important.

You can prepare yourself to speak with a strong voice with these exercises:

- Lie on the floor. Breathe in through your nose, focusing your breath down to your abdomen. Place one hand on your stomach and focus on the expansion and contraction. Breathe in again slowly, focusing on the expansion, then breathe out (through your mouth with rounded lips), focusing on the contraction. Repeat this breathing pattern five times.

- Breathe in again to the count of five, and then exhale on "mmmmm" for five counts. Repeat five times.

- Breathe in on a count of five, and exhale on "mmmmmmmmmaaaah" alternating between "mmmm" and "ahh" (notice as you move from the "mmmm" to the "aah" how the nasal vibrations stop).

- Breathe in and then exhale on "aaah"

(without the "mmmmm"). Keep your mouth open wide, with your jaw relaxed.

(Special thanks to Paul Michaels, a speech-language pathologist and member of the Corporate Speech Solutions team, for contributing the preceding voice exercises.)

- Practice using nasal resonance to focus your voice forward. Practice the following phrases/sentences from *Talking Business: When English is Your Second Language* by Jayne Latz and Stacey Rimikis. Repeat each phrase three times each, emphasizing the "m" and "n" sounds:

    – Mike might move to Mexico.

    – My mom mends men's clothing.

    – Nick needs a knife now.

    – I noticed Nora's new necklace.

    – No one knows her name.

    – The magic mirror is in the middle.

    – Mitch and Marie met at the movies.

    – It's normal to nap at noon.

    – We know no one is nearby.

    – Mark meant to marry a model.

- Practice breath control. Relax, inhale deeply, breathing from your stomach, and count to fifteen as you exhale. Try to exhale for slightly longer each time you repeat the exercise.

In order to use your vocal volume to communicate to the best of your ability, you must first be able to manipulate it effectively. One way to learn this is by vocal exercises. Choose a neutral phrase, for example, "My name is Jayne." To begin, simply practice saying the phrase at varying volumes, starting at a whisper and gradually building to a shout. Then take a moment and jot down a few different situations in which you may need to monitor your volume; for example, speaking quietly to a colleague at his cubicle, calling to a friend across a crowded cafeteria, whispering to the person next to you during a meeting, or speaking with your boss one-on-one at her desk. Then practice saying your neutral phrase as though you were in each of these situations. To help you get started, consider what volume may be needed for each of the following situations:

- You are in the library and don't want to disturb the other people in the room.

- You are speaking to an elderly man who has trouble hearing.

- You are at a business dinner in a noisy restaurant, speaking to someone at the other end of the large table.

- You are speaking on the telephone, and you can hear a fire engine passing by the window of your listener.

- You are speaking to a group of thirty-five without a microphone.

Continue to modify your volume until you feel you've reached a comfortable level for each situation, and mentally note how that volume sounds and feels. With practice, volume modification will become second nature.

## Clear Speech

 Enunciation, or the precise pronunciation of speech sounds, is critical to projecting professionalism and confidence. One common mistake in business communication is not separating your day-to-day speech from your professional speech. When talking casually in everyday situations, we tend to run our words together as we speak. For example, "would've" and "should've" become "wudda" and "shudda." "Want to" and "going to" become "wanna" and "gonna." Although this manner of speaking may be acceptable among friends and acquaintances, professional business speech should be more clear and enunciated. Asking a friend, "Didjeet?" *(Did you eat?)* may be completely acceptable. However, when speaking with a business contact, "Have you eaten?" sounds much more professional and polished.

It's remarkable how much more intelligent and professional speech can sound when properly enunciated. Slurring your words together and omitting syllables creates an impression of sloppiness and laziness. Take some time and honestly evaluate how clear and crisp your speech is. It may help to record yourself the next time you are on a business call. As you replay the recording, listen to your speech and decide if you are pronouncing each sound of each word. If the answer is no, you may need to put some time into refining your manner of speaking. Take note of some phrases you typically use on a day-to-day basis and practice saying them when you are alone, taking care to produce each sound and syllable. Developing clear speech will take time and effort, but the results are well worth it.

## Enunciation Practice

Producing all of the sounds of a word in a crisp, articulate manner may take practice if you are a habitual mumbler. Read each of the words, phrases and sentences below, carefully producing each sound and paying particular attention to the consonants at the end of each word. Keep in mind that there is a big difference between the numbers thirty and thirteen and not pronouncing the word clearly can lead to a costly mistake.

**Numbers**

one

two

three

four

five

six

seven

eight

nine

ten

eleven

twelve

thirteen

thirty

forty

fourteen

fifty

fifteen

sixty

sixteen

seventy

seventeen

eighty

eighteen

ninety

nineteen

## One-syllable Words

meet

put

pack

read

write

act

waste

like

room

tell

pen

miss

Have you ever heard someone pronounce the word governor as "govner?" Or probably as "probly"? This is often caused when people are speaking quickly and casually. However, if the words are industry specific and the listener is not necessarily familiar with them, the dropped syllable can cause misunderstanding and miscommunication. Practice saying each syllable in the words below.

**Multi-syllabic Words**

connect

attract

conceal

create

present

probably

concentrate

financial

enunciate

remedial

judgmental

contradictory

phenomenal

publication

credibility

judicial

procrastination

uninhibited

# Accent Reduction

Many people consider their accent a part of their identity, an indicator of where they come from and who they are. However, there are others who would love nothing more than to tone down the regional distinction. For example, as a company based in New York City, we at Corporate Speech Solutions receive numerous requests for modifying the infamous "New Yawk" accent.

Accent reduction isn't for everybody; many people have strong, identifiable accents and consider them a positive aspect of their communication style. However, for many people, an accent can negatively impact communication. In some cases, the accent is so strong that others, particularly those who are non-native speakers of the language, have trouble understanding the message. In other cases, people may feel that the accent projects a certain stereotype or image. If the accent is particularly distinct, people may be distracted and focus more on the person's speech than his message. When this is the case, and a person seeks to reduce his American regional accent, the goal is usually Standard American English (SAE), the "accentless accent."

Standard American English is a type of English speech that sounds identifiably American but has no particular regional accent. This is the type of speech you might hear when listening to your average American newscaster or broadcast journalist.

Maintaining the integrity of the accent is important to each individual's cultural identity. My goal in working with clients is to build clarity and confidence in their day-to-day business interactions by focusing on sounds and intonation patterns that interfere with listener intelligibility. Throughout the training, progress is reported by the client in one of two ways: the reduced number of daily requests to repeat what was said and the reported feeling of increased confidence.

If you would like to modify your regional accent and tailor your speech more closely to Standard American English, do some research into the hallmarks of your particular accent. For example, the following are common aspects of the New York regional accent:

- Dropped "r" sounds, especially at the end of words (e.g., "better" becomes "betta") or before a consonant (e.g., "card" becomes "cahd")

- "R" sounds appearing in words that have no "r", often after a vowel at the end of a word (e.g., "idea" becomes "idear")

- "Th" sounds changed to "d" sounds (e.g., "this" and "that" become "dis" and "dat")

- The short "a" sound changed to a diphthong that sounds more like "ee-yah" (e.g., "cab" may sound closer to "keeyab")

- The "aw" sound drawn out and more rounded than in Standard American English (e.g., "coffee" may be pronounced as "cawwfee")

- Rapid rate of speech and lack of space between words, as in the infamous "Fugged-aboudit" (Forget about it) or "djeet?" (Did you eat?)

- Hypernasality (i.e., "talking through your nose")

Once you've pinpointed the identifying hallmarks of your accent, you can work to systematically reduce or eliminate them. In order to avoid becoming frustrated or overwhelmed, target only one aspect of your speech at a time, beginning with those you feel would be the easiest to modify. Once you feel you've mastered one, then move on to the next until you've tackled each item on your list. It may help to record yourself before you begin to attempt accent reduction, and then at periodic points throughout, in order to track your progress.

If you find that you are having particular difficulty modifying your speech, a variety of materials exist that can make the task easier. For example, the Corporate Speech Solutions workbook titled *Talking Business: When English Is Your Second Language*, provides in-depth information on each individual sound of Standard American English, as well as words and sentences for practice with professional audio recordings of a Standard American English accent modeling each. This type of tool that breaks down individual speech sounds may help you to more accurately fine-tune your speech and reduce your accent in a more systematic way.

## Practice

As professional speech and communication coaches, we at Corporate Speech Solutions have the opportunity to see clients use the techniques we've discussed to make phenomenal progress in their professional speaking skills. However, all too often, this success remains within the confines of our sessions, and clients find that their new-found speech and communication skills don't carry over into their daily life. This is because, like any other skill set, speech and communication must be practiced regularly to be fully learned. Without practice, your brain and body don't become fully accustomed to the new skill. However, when you repeatedly perform an activity on a regular basis, your neural pathways and muscle groups begin to perform the activity more automatically, requiring less active thought from you.

In order to practice your speech techniques effectively, a combination of direct and indirect practice is recommended.

**Direct practice:** Direct practice involves time exclusively dedicated to honing your communicative skills. It may include some of the suggestions that have been put forth throughout this book; for example, video or audio recording yourself and reviewing the material or asking others to provide feedback. Direct practice may also involve drills or exercises designed to systematically improve your skills. Over the years we have created materials that provide audio and visual feedback to help facilitate success.  Direct practice is usually most effective in the early stages of learning a new skill. You may also use direct practice as a method to brush up your skills before a situation in which good personal communication is particularly important (e.g., a business meeting or important phone call). Use some advance preparation in these situations, and set aside time beforehand to sit down and work on your communication skills. Use a mirror and a recorder and practice what you are going to say, paying particular attention to your volume, rate of speech and clear pronunciation.

**Indirect practice:** Indirect practice involves integrating practice into your daily life. Once you've pinned down the basics through direct practice, indirect practice provides the opportunity to generalize your skills in your everyday interactions and utilize them in a more functional context. One way to integrate indirect practice into your life is to choose a specific time or event in your daily routine and consciously use it to work on your targeted skill.

You will want to choose a time that involves good communicative opportunities, such as a meeting or returning phone calls. You will most likely want to avoid overly stressful communication exchanges (e.g., one-on-one meetings with your boss or high-stakes presentations). Although you clearly want to utilize good communication techniques during these events, using them as a time to consciously focus on communicative skills may take your mental focus away from the content of your message. One great indirect method of practice I share with all my clients that have young children is reading to their children each night. The children's book might have five to fifteen words on a page making it quite easy to concentrate on the sounds being practiced. It is a win-win situation; you have time to practice and your child is delighted to have you read to them.

You can also use the following ideas to help you practice your speech as you go about your day:

- Leave notes for yourself in places that you will see often throughout the day. For example, put a Post-it note on your phone that says "Slow down" or "Clear and precise." Then, each time you pick up your phone to speak with someone, you will encounter that visual reminder and focus on that specific skill.

- Choose a point during your day when you will take five minutes and think about your communication skills. Take note of any problems you feel you may have had and quickly jot them down on a piece of paper. Then, make a brief mental plan to avoid making these same mistakes for the rest of the day. Make this "communication-check date" with yourself a part of your daily routine.

In addition to practicing general communication skills, you may also want to rehearse your public speaking skills in a low-stress environment to help you become more comfortable when a high-stakes professional public speaking event arises. Look for the following opportunities to practice your public speaking skills:

**In your non-professional life:** Whether it is at your church or temple, your children's school, or a social club, there are often opportunities in your personal life to speak in front of others. Volunteer for positions and events that involve speaking or presenting to a group to practice your communication skills in a low-stress, non-professional situation.

**In social situations:** Even casual social gatherings can provide valuable opportunities to practice your public speaking skills. Use the tools and tips you've learned, even in informal speaking situations; for example, telling a story to a group of friends at a party. The more you focus on these techniques, the more naturally they will come.

**At work:** Even if your job doesn't involve speaking in front of others on a regular basis, opportunities can often be found with a little digging. Volunteer to speak at meetings or to give informal internal presentations. If you have the chance, attend networking events where you will have the opportunity to practice your introduction when speaking to potential clients and customers.

The more often you practice, the more automatic good speech will become. Over time you will find that proper speech and good communication habits no longer require conscious effort on your part. Remember: Use it or lose it.

# CHAPTER 4

# The Second Step: Communicating with Clarity and Confidence

Confidence is a key component in creating a strong, capable professional image. When communicating in a professional setting, projecting confidence can have a significant impact on how others perceive your character and professional abilities. Those who appear confident are often assumed to be more capable in their jobs and more worthy of trust and respect. While a lucky few may naturally project a confident air, the majority of us must work to develop this skill. This chapter will provide you with tips for developing the confident communication skills you need to succeed in the workplace. Through non-verbal communication techniques and strategies as well as speech improvement exercises, this section of the book will help mold your speech, language, and overall business communication so that you can communicate with clarity and confidence.

## Body Language

Often people are so focused on what it is they're
saying that they lose sight of the fact that the way
they move and hold themselves can communicate
just as much as their words. In fact, according to
some studies, up to 93 percent of communication
is nonverbal. Your listener is able to gain a great
deal of information simply by observing the way
that you move, gesture, and hold your body. Take
note of your listeners' body language as well; their
nonverbal communication can speak volumes about
how they're receiving your message.

By paying attention to your body language, you
can craft an image that projects confidence and
professionalism. Take a short video of yourself either
giving a presentation or engaging in natural speech.
Then, use the following checklist to evaluate your
body language:

- Are you smiling?

- Are you connecting to your listener with
  your eyes, or looking at the ceiling, the floor,
  or your smartphone?

- Are you anxiously scratching your arm or
  neck?

- Are you playing with your hair (ladies)?

- Is your hand in your pocket?

This checklist is a great start, but remember to keep an eye out for any other body language idiosyncrasies that may negatively impact your image.

## Posture

One important aspect of body language is posture. The way in which you hold yourself can speak volumes about how you perceive yourself and the value of your message. Unfortunately, posture is often a deeply engrained habit formed over many years, which makes it particularly challenging to change. However, with some conscious effort, you can gradually modify your posture and use it to project a strong, confident professional image.

So what exactly is the ideal posture? Rounded shoulders and slouching can make you appear unsure of yourself or unprofessional. On the other hand, standing too rigidly can make you appear ill at ease and tense. The goal is to achieve a posture that falls between these two extremes. To do this, start by standing straight with your shoulders held slightly back. Orient your head so that your chin is level with the floor—you should be looking neither up nor down at your listener, but straight at them. You should also face your listener with your hips and chest so as to appear fully engaged in the conversation. In order to maintain this position, imagine a string running from your tailbone, through your spine, and emerging from the top of your head. Now, imagine a force from above gently pulling on that string until you are perfectly aligned.

When standing and speaking with someone, it's not only your posture that affects your image, but your stance as well. Stand with your feet roughly shoulder-width apart, with your weight evenly distributed. Maintain an even stance, and avoid shifting your weight from foot to foot. Fidgeting or leaning against an object can make you appear to be overly casual and unprofessional.

Putting conscious thought into your posture can help achieve an ideal position, but it can also feel and look unnatural when too much thought is employed. Simultaneously improving your posture and remaining natural requires some practice. Once you've found your best posture, take a moment to relax while remaining in the position. Avoid muscle tension and keep your breathing even. Finding a balance between conscious effort and relaxation will help you to maintain a natural posture which projects confidence and self-assurance.

If you feel that your posture is an area of weakness for you and needs serious work, take some time and practice achieving the ideal alignment in the mirror, both standing and sitting. Have someone take a short video of you delivering a brief presentation.

We use a ten-point scale to assess our clients from
head to toe, but you can ask a trusted colleague
for feedback. Once you feel that you look strong,
but natural, close your eyes and take note of how
your body *feels*. Focus on the positioning of your
body parts in relation to one another. By mentally
recording the physical sense of strong posture, you
can more easily achieve it when you don't have a
mirror to provide that visual feedback.

Breaking deeply engrained habits of posture can be a
challenge, but taking the time to consciously change
your physical presentation is worth the effort. With
continued practice, your new, more confident
posture will eventually become second nature.

## Eye Contact

How you meet your speaking partner's gaze in
conversation can play a huge role in how he or she
perceives you. Developing the right pattern of eye
contact is crucial in projecting confidence. The most
effortless way to improve your eye contact is to truly
listen to what your conversation partner is saying.
When you are genuinely absorbed in a conversation,
proper eye contact becomes natural. However, in
some situations, especially those that are stressful
or emotional, you may need to put in some effort to
achieve a good level of eye contact.

When it comes to the amount and intensity of eye contact in an interaction, it's important to try to strike a balance. Failing to make steady eye contact and frequently averting your eyes from the person you are speaking with can project insecurity, boredom, or even submissiveness. However, if you stare too intently into another person's eyes, you can appear overly intense and uncomfortable. Instead, aim for direct eye contact approximately 80 percent of the time. This equates to briefly shifting your gaze for one second after every four seconds of eye contact. Easier translation, finish your thought by looking at the person and then briefly look away. The way in which you shift your gaze is also important. As you look away, look up or to the side rather than down. Looking down is a sign of insecurity. By looking up or sideways, you'll appear to be thinking about what is being said rather than averting your gaze purposefully.

You can also use eye contact to project confidence when speaking to a group or giving a presentation. When speaking in front of a group, many people will simply gaze above the heads of the audience members or focus on an object in the distance. However, this creates a lack of connection with your audience and gives the impression that you are uneasy. Instead, make eye contact with individual members of the audience for about three seconds per person. Vary this so that you're looking at people in different parts of the room, so that the entire group feels as though they've connected with you. Every so often, allow your eyes to sweep across the crowd. The combination of individual and group attention will help to create a feeling of intimacy combined with professionalism. The important takeaway is not to glance at the spot in the back of the room or on the wall. Look at the people you are speaking with and let them know you are speaking to them. Whenever I speak to a group of twenty to thirty people, I ask for a show of hands by anyone that feels I have not connected with them with my eyes during the presentation. No one ever raises his or her hand.

Keep in mind, what is considered appropriate eye contact may vary between cultures. Chapter 7 provides more in-depth information on multicultural considerations on verbal and nonverbal communication.

## Gesture

The ways in which you use your hands in conversation can make or break the image you project to others. Study after study has suggested that gestures can play an enormous role in what your listener receives from your message. For example, in one study, people who gestured with their palms facing upward were judged to have a sense of openness and honesty. Those who subtly made a prayer position with their hands (palms together, fingers facing upward) when making a request were perceived to be more sincere and were more likely to receive what they were asking for. While not all of your gestures need be so specific or calculated, this does tell us that what you do with your hands can greatly impact your message. Be aware of how you are gesturing while you speak and whether or not your gestures are consistent with the message you are trying to get across.

The way in which you use your hands should vary depending on your role within the conversation. While listening, it's best to let your hands rest comfortably, either at your sides or on the table in front of you. Often people fidget—twirling their hair, toying with a ring or a pen, playing with items on their desk—without even realizing it. This can create the impression that you are nervous or disinterested. Once again, here is where a video recording can come in handy. You may be completely unaware of how often you are fidgeting. Check in with yourself every so often in conversation and take note of how your hands are behaving.

When speaking, you should be using your hands to gesture naturally, complimenting your speech and projecting an air of confidence and control. Often people are uncomfortable using their hands when they speak and fall into default positions that limit their movement. While this may be suitable on occasion, continually lapsing into a fixed position will make you appear immobile and insecure. In particular, the following habits can be particularly harmful:

*Sitting with your chin in your hands:* This casual posture makes you look overly relaxed. Since it's also a position often associated with childhood, you may appear inexperienced or unprofessional in comparison with those around you.

*Folding your arms:* The person who takes up the most physical space in a contained group setting is generally perceived to be dominant over his or her peers. Habitually folding your arms creates the impression you're trying to take up as little space as possible and fade into the background. This creates an air of passivity and uncertainty.

Instead of allowing yourself to fall into a fixed posture like those above, become comfortable utilizing gestures. Not only do natural gestures make you appear confident and at ease, they can also be used to draw attention to important points in your speech. Making subtle but definite gestures during key moments will help your listener focus on these points. One movement that works particularly well is gesturing toward your listener with your palm facing upwards. The forward motion signals strength and security, while your upturned palm projects openness and honesty.

To get a good sense of how you gesture on a regular basis, ask a friend or close coworker to keep an eye on how you move during a typical interaction and provide feedback. Once you're aware of your personal patterns, it's much easier to shape them to the image you want to project.

### The Handshake

It is said that one establishes an opinion of another person within the first five seconds of meeting them. One symbolic action that takes place during this time is the introductory handshake. What does your handshake say about you and how can you improve it?

One important rule is to make verbal contact before you make physical contact. You should never shake hands silently. As you reach for the person's hand, introduce yourself (e.g., "Hi, I'm Mike."). Or, if someone else has made the introduction for you, offer a word of greeting (e.g., "Nice to meet you," or "It's a pleasure meeting you.").

Another important aspect of the perfect handshake is the grip. No one likes to shake a limp hand—it comes across as passive and disinterested. However, a handshake that is too firm may seem aggressive or uncomfortable. Practice lightly squeezing your own forearm to gauge how strong a grip is comfortable and how it feels to you. Strive for pressure that is firm, but relaxed.

It is also vital that a handshake last for the right amount of time. A typical handshake should last approximately three to four seconds. This allows enough time to make a connection, but doesn't last long enough to feel awkward. During this time, you also want to achieve the right motion. Don't simply hold the other person's hand; lightly pump their hand up and down two to three times, leading from the elbow. Again, moderation is key; remaining motionless is awkward, but aggressively pulling your partner's hand up and down is equally uncomfortable.

Finally, always look people in the eye as you shake hands. You aren't simply performing a gesture; you are making a connection with another human being. Avoiding eye contact makes the handshake seem insincere and meaningless. Maintaining eye contact allows you to appear confident and amiable. And don't forget to smile.

## Reading Body Language

Once you've cultivated your own nonverbal communication to reflect confidence and professionalism, there's still another aspect of nonverbal communication to consider: reading the body language of others. In addition to being mindful of your own nonverbal communication, you should closely monitor that of your listener as well. If your conversation partner is confused, bored, or upset, he may not say so directly, but his body language will usually do the talking for him.

When gauging another person's nonverbal communication, it's crucial to consider all of the different aspects of their body language as a whole. For example, crossed arms may indicate a variety of emotions, but if you take other body language into account, it's easier to determine what your communication partner is feeling. For example, crossed arms and a downward or sideways gaze often indicate discomfort with the topic or situation at hand. However, if crossed arms are accompanied by direct, somewhat intense eye contact, feelings of hostility are likely.

Use your conversation partner's body language to your advantage. Pay close attention to facial expressions and body language to see how your message is being received and then tailor your speech and message accordingly. Reading between the lines can go a long way toward fixing communication problems before they begin.

## Clear, Confident Speech

Everyone has particular speech habits that characterize the way they communicate. Often these are neither good nor bad, but simply personal hallmarks of an individual's speech. However, certain speech quirks can convey a lack of confidence and professionalism. On April 24, 2013 *The Wall Street Journal* published an article titled "Is This How You Really Talk?" which revealed that the sound of a speaker's voice matters twice as much as the content of the message.

One pattern that can be particularly damaging is speaking with a rising intonation at the end of each sentence so that statements sound like questions (this is the speech habit I described in the beginning of the book when discussing my friend, Jennifer).

This gives off an air of insecurity and makes it seem that you are unsure of yourself and seeking your listener's approval. Avoid this pattern at all costs, and end each sentence authoritatively.

Another common speech pattern that can betray a lack of confidence is overusing question words such as "right," "okay," or "you know" at the end of sentences. Although these phrases are warranted in certain situations, using them consistently makes it seem as though you are not fully confident in your message and require constant validation from others.

Recently we began working with a high-level polished professional whose boss hired us to eliminate his excessive use of phrases such as "sort of" and "kind of." As a compliance officer, he felt, and rightfully so, that saying "we sort of need to be compliant" is not very professional and doesn't communicate a confidant style.

Display confident speech by using a strong, dynamic voice that engages the listener.

Exactly how do you go about engaging the listener? By varying the tone of your voice. Some people mistakenly equate a lack of intonational variety with professionalism, thinking it makes them sound sober and serious. However, the result is more often dull, monotone speech. This type of speech conveys disinterest and a lack of enthusiasm for the topic.

In some situations, this can be problematic to the point of interfering with professional goals. Several years ago a client enrolled in speech-improvement services because, while interviewing for a job, the HR recruiter told him that one reason he was not getting called back was due to his monotone voice. Speaking with varied intonation keeps your listener engaged and makes your speech far more interesting to listen to.

## Intonation Practice

Read the following list of phrases out loud. Read each phrase three times, using a different intonation pattern from the list below each time.

1. Will the meeting start later than expected?

2. I thought he was going to be here at three o'clock.

3. Are you completely sure the information is correct?

4. Let's take another look at those numbers after lunch.

5. I think it would be better if we saved this conversation for another time.

6. You're saying that you never received last week's report?

7.  The results from last quarter are completely different from what I expected.

8.  I haven't spoken to Susan from accounting in over a week.

9.  I really need to talk to you after the meeting this afternoon.

10. The CEO's presentation next Thursday is mandatory.

Demanding

Impatient

Concerned

Confident

Disappointed

Confused

Irritated

Bored

Pleased

Embarrassed

Impressed

Excited

**Fillers**

Another speech habit that can be fatal to projecting confidence is the use of filler words. People often pepper their speech with words such as "um," "uh," or "you know," which contain no content, add nothing to the message, and interrupt the flow of speech. Some of the most common filler patterns include:

- Using "you know" in rapid or spontaneous speech

- Ending sentences with, "Okay?" "Right?" "See?" or "You know what I mean?"

- Using "Um" at the beginning of sentences, when transitioning from one thought to another, or before a list of items

These filler patterns can make you sound inexperienced or even unintelligent.

Learning to speak without fillers may appear to be a difficult task, but one worth undertaking. Use the following four steps to identify and eliminate filler words from your speech.

**Step 1: Awareness**

Before you can take steps to reduce your filler words, you must first be aware of them. One great way to do this is to record yourself as you speak. Use a recorder and speak about a topic on which you are comfortable and knowledgeable. For example, talk about what you do in a typical day of work or where you went and what you did on your last vacation. Try to speak as naturally as possible, as though you were speaking to a colleague. Record yourself for one to two minutes. You may be amazed at how many more filler words you are using than you thought.

As you listen to your recording, count how many filler words you used. You should be using no more than one filler word per minute. Sorry, but if you use filler words more frequently than this, you risk distracting your audience and confusing your message. After you've identified your filler words, take a moment and jot down the sentences in which they were used. Then take a moment to say these sentences aloud with the filler words removed. Note the difference between the two sentences, and how the sentence with no filler words sounds stronger, more professional, and more confident.

## Step 2: Recognizing your personal patterns

Each person has a particular pattern when it comes to filler words. In reducing your reliance on fillers, it helps to be aware of which filler words you use most often. The same recording created in Step 1 can be used in this step as well. Listen to the recording again, write down the specific fillers you used, then tally them to see which fillers you use most often. For example, you may find that you interject the word "like" several times in each sentence, or that you say "um" whenever there's a break in the flow of your speech.

Once you have recognized which filler words you use most often, try to identify the situations in which you are most likely to use them. Some people start every sentence with "um" while others insert a filler such as "um" as soon as they stop to think. Many others find that they use filler words most often when feeling anxious or excited. Once you have recognized in which situations you are more likely to use fillers, you can take extra care to monitor your speech in those situations.

## Step 3: Anticipate
Using the information you gathered from Steps 1 and 2, you should now be able to anticipate when you will most likely use filler words as well as which ones you most commonly use. This anticipation is a key tool in filler word reduction. In order to use it to your advantage, begin by choosing a specific time in your daily routine in which you will be particularly conscious of your filler word usage. For example, you may choose a meeting with your colleagues or the time in which you return your voicemails. Whichever situation you select, during this period,

closely monitor your speech and take note of when you feel tempted to use a filler word.

## Step 4: Silence

Once you have noted that you are tempted to use a filler word, simply pause instead. Most people feel self-conscious using silence in a conversation, but a well-timed pause sounds far more professional and confident than filling the silence with fillers like "um" and "well." When you are tempted to use a filler word, simply stop for a moment. This will give you the opportunity to gather your thoughts. In addition, it gives your listener the chance to process your message, helping to make your speech more comprehensible. The pause is the magic to your message.

While too many filler words will negatively impact your message, completely eliminating them from your vocabulary may be unrealistic. At Corporate Speech Solutions, our barometer for acceptable filler word use is no more than two filler words per every two minutes. Everyone tends to use one of these words from time to time, but going beyond this threshold and using more than two filler words in two minutes will have an impact on your business communication skills. You will sound less confident and less professional.

Using filler words is a difficult habit to break for many speakers, but it is worth the time and effort to lessen your dependence on them. Fillers can completely derail the confident image that you have worked so hard to perfect. Using this four-step process, you can reduce your filler word usage and improve the fluency and professionalism of your speech.

# CHAPTER 5

# The Third Step: Standing Out in the Corporate World

There are some communication strategies that are vital to any interaction. Then there are those that lend themselves to particular, professional situations. In this chapter, learn to utilize communication skills to navigate business-specific situations and increase your professional prowess.

## Meetings

*"A meeting is an event where minutes are taken and hours wasted."* — UNKNOWN

While meetings are a necessary part of nearly every business, all too often they become drawn-out, ineffective wastes of time and money. However, a well-run meeting can be a great tool for developing and exchanging ideas. What makes the difference between a waste of time and an effective meeting of the minds? Communication.

**Communicate your goals:** Well before the meeting takes place, make sure that not only the topic is set, but the specific goals of the meeting as well. Then, include these in a memo for everyone attending. If all parties are aware of exactly what you are hoping to achieve, they will be mentally better prepared and will be able to more effectively contribute to the conversation.

**Make the agenda known:** As the meeting begins, review the goals that you would like to achieve. Then establish a set time frame in which you would like to address them. If everyone is aware in advance of how much time you expect to devote to each topic, it will be much easier to keep your schedule on track.

**Be concise:** Every office has one—that person who habitually goes on and on in meetings, making it hard for anyone else to get a word in. While you don't want to discourage people like this (they often have excellent ideas buried in all that speech), you must put a limit on how much they speak in order to allow an effective flow of communication. In order to politely move along, jump in and say, "I really like what you're saying, and it sounds like you have some great ideas. Unfortunately, we're in a bit of a time crunch, but if you'd like, we can meet later on and discuss some of your thoughts."

**Speak effectively:** When speaking in a business meeting, be aware of the two big Cs: clear and concise. When speaking to a group of people who may have very different communication styles, it's important to keep your message as clear and simple as possible in order to avoid miscommunications and confusion. Being concise is equally important; meetings that drag on and on are everyone's worst nightmare. When speaking in a meeting, make sure you are making your point in the shortest, most direct way possible. In 2015 Corporate Speech Solutions conducted a survey. Nearly half of the respondents reported that people who seem to talk and talk but never get to the point are their biggest communication pet peeve.

**Open ears, open mind:** Often people spend their time in meetings planning out what they want to contribute to the conversation. While it's important to put some thought into what you want to say, this can often lead to missing the contributions of others. Make sure to really listen when someone is speaking, rather than just making eye contact and nodding while plotting your next discussion point. To keep your focus, continually recap in your mind the key points of what the speaker is saying.

**Don't be afraid to ask questions:** Despite everyone's best efforts, communication breakdowns are inevitable. If you don't fully understand someone's point or have missed a key part of their idea, don't be afraid to ask questions or request clarification. Odds are if something is unclear to you, there is at least one other person in the room who is confused as well.

## Networking

Making connections in the business world is crucial to success. Whether you're an individual working for a large corporation, a business owner, or anything in between, everyone can benefit from networking. However, to successfully network, you must do more than simply make the acquaintance of others in your field. Effective, professional networking is a skill that must be worked on and developed. I have already discussed several strategies to use in all networking situations. Introducing yourself with a strong hand-shake paired with a clear introduction of your name and company is a great first step. Take a look at the following tips to help you learn to put your best networking foot forward:

**Use all available avenues:** People sometimes restrict themselves to the type of networking they are most comfortable with. For example, technophobes will often avoid virtual networking, while more reserved individuals will shy away from large conventions. Make the effort to go outside your comfort zone and utilize as many networking avenues as possible. The type of contacts you will make in each setting are often entirely different from one another and can benefit you or your company in different ways.

**Help your colleagues:** Even though you may not benefit immediately, make the effort to introduce those within your circle to contacts that may be useful for them. The professional world can be surprisingly small, and the colleague you help to make a connection today may run into a perfect networking opportunity for you in the future.

**Avoid the sales pitch:** While you certainly want potential contacts to understand what it is you have to offer, no one wants to feel as if they are being sold something right off the bat. Many people lose out on excellent networking opportunities by coming on too strong and appearing abrasive and overly aggressive. Remember to ask the person you are meeting questions about what they do and what brings them to the event rather than dominate the conversation. Don't push your business card in their hand unless they ask. Why waste paper? Establish a pleasant social relationship as you network to improve the possibility of a successful professional connection. You never know—that professional may become a good friend.

## Small Talk

The Stanford University School of Business conducted a study that tracked MBA students twenty years after graduation to determine different factors that may affect success ("Predictors of Business Success Over Two Decades: An MBA Longitudinal Study" by Bradley A. Hanson, Thomas W. Harrell, Working Paper No. 788, 1985). The result? One of the most important keys to success seemed to be the ability to converse well with others.

Often people regard small talk as a waste of time. However, being able to discuss ordinary, non-business-related topics with colleagues and clients plays an important role in your professional life and can greatly increase your success in networking.

This past year, more than ever before, my clients indicated a concern with making small talk. At first I thought it was only my international professionals expressing this concern but later it was apparent that many professionals struggle with small talk. Making small talk allows you to connect with others on a more human level, helping to forge a deeper professional relationship. The trick is to find the happy medium of being friendly and open while remaining professional. Learn to master the art of small talk with the following tips:

**Prepare yourself:** Take some time to prepare some generic questions that you can keep in your arsenal in case you find yourself needing to make small talk on the spot. Weather, travel, and current events are always great topics. If you are going to an event where you anticipate meeting many new people, think of questions that may specifically be geared to that group or event. Consider the type of business most attendees are a part of, where they are from, and what their interests may be.

**Be a good listener:** Maintain eye contact with your conversation partner rather than scanning the room as you listen. Give indications that you are listening to your partner by nodding and adding in occasional short responses such as "Really?" or "Uh-huh." And most important: never, never interrupt.

**Use the Ws:** If you find yourself at a loss for what to say, run through the "five Ws and one H" in your mind: "who," "what," "when," "where," "why," and "how." Usually you can spark a conversation by asking a basic, open-ended question with one of these words. For example:

- "Who do you know here?"

- "When was the last time you visited New York?"

- "How long have you known so-and-so?"

- What brings you here?

**Know when to walk away:** At some point your conversation may hit an uncomfortable lull as you and your conversation partner run out of things to talk about. Rather than force the conversation, politely excuse yourself. Make your exit as graceful and natural as possible. Saying that you need to say hello to a colleague, get a drink, or step outside for some air are all reliable exit lines.

## Conversation Starters

Even if you have excellent communication skills, striking up a conversation with someone you'd like to speak to can often be awkward or uncomfortable if you are unprepared. Use the following tips and phrases to get the conversational ball rolling.

**General tips:** Place yourself so you are near the person you would like to speak to. Then wait until he or she looks your way, make eye contact, and smile. This shows your intent to speak with the person and opens up the possibility of a conversation. Keep your body language open: face your target with your shoulders and avoid crossing your arms or legs.

To join a group having a conversation, stand at the periphery of the group you would like to join and make eye contact with several of the speakers in the group. In most cases, someone will back up slightly to allow you to join. Wait for an appropriate moment, and ask a question of the person speaking about the topic at hand. It will make you appear friendly and open to new ideas.

**Conversation starters for starting a specific discussion:**

"I've been meaning to talk with you about…"

"Do you have a minute to discuss…"

"When you have a moment, I'd love to get your opinion on…"

"If you don't mind, I'd like to bounce a few ideas off of you about…"

**Conversation starters to speak to an individual already in a group:**

"Could I steal you away for a moment to discuss…"

"I hate to interrupt, but I've been meaning to talk to you about…"

"May I borrow you for a second? I was hoping we could chat about…"

**Conversation starters for strangers at a networking event or conference:**

"What business/industry are you in?"

"How did you get into (industry/business)?"

"Who are you looking to connect with today?"

"Have you been to (current city) before?"

"What do you think of (hotel, city, food, etc.)?"

## The Elevator Pitch

Ideally, we'd all like to be able to invest significant time in networking and developing professional relationships. Unfortunately, reality tends to get in the way, and many professional interactions and first impressions are cut short. This is why every professional needs to develop a strong elevator pitch: a short summary of who you are, what you do, and why the person you are talking to should care. Your pitch should communicate the benefits you bring to the client, not all the services you provide. The goal is to get the listener interested so that they want to ask for your business card and learn more at another time. Too often we attend networking events where people are asked to introduce themselves in sixty seconds. Instead of engaging the listener, the listener often tunes out or looks at their smartphone. In order to craft an elevator pitch that is effective and engaging, use the A.I.D.E. (attention, introduction, description, ending) formula:

**Attention:** Begin your elevator pitch with a question, quote, or anecdote that applies to your line of work to grab your audience's attention and engage your listeners. For example, as a corporate speech coach, I may say: "How many of you have ever received a voicemail message that you needed to replay once, twice, maybe three times just to get the person's name that called?"

**Introduction:** Once you have their attention you are now ready to introduce yourself and your company. Make sure to speak particularly clearly and slowly during your introduction, pausing between your first and last name as well as your company name to ensure your audience fully understands this information.

**Description:** Briefly describe what you do or what you would like to share with your audience. To craft a strong description, consider the following questions: What makes you different? How do you stand out? What benefit do you bring to the audience?

**Ending:** Bring your pitch to a close by inviting the audience to approach or contact you for more information, and restate your name and company. Restating your name and company name is crucial. Many people may not have heard your name in the beginning but as you described your product or service they became interested. If you don't restate your information they may never be able to contact you.

**Remember:** Always communicate with clarity and confidence.

- Power up your voice so the audience can hear what you have to say.

- Be clear and articulate. Pronounce every sound of every word.

- Don't rush. Maintain a rate that is energetic, but slow enough to be clear.

- Avoid filler words such as "um" and "like." They cloud your message and make you sound inarticulate.

# Telecommunication

As mentioned earlier, up to 93 percent of communication is nonverbal. In daily communication, this means that your facial expressions, gestures, eye contact, and overall body language play a huge role in helping your listener to understand your message. However, when speaking on the telephone, none of these visual cues are available to you or your listener, leaving nothing but your words to carry your message.

The most important rule for understandable telephone communication is also the simplest: speak slowly and clearly. Many people are unsure of their telephone communication skills; because of this, they feel nervous and speak rapidly, making their speech even more difficult to understand. During telephone conversations, make an effort to speak a little more slowly than usual, and make sure that you are pronouncing each sound of every word.

Even though your listener cannot see your face, smiling and using other appropriate facial expressions can improve your message. Using a variety of facial expressions helps improve your intonation, making your message more relatable and engaging.

Although posture may not seem important in a situation in which your listener cannot see you, strong posture is important when using the telephone. Posture is not only a visual cue, but can greatly impact your speech as well. Never conduct an important telephone call while lying down or slouching in your chair. Bad posture can decrease your breath support, making your speech weaker and less intelligible. In addition, good posture helps you remain alert and helps you to concentrate on your speech.

Keeping your message clear and concise is also important. Try writing down the important points of what you want to say to your listener in advance to help you maintain a clear message. However, avoid writing down what you want to say word for word. This can tempt you to read directly from the page, decreasing your expression and intonation, and decreasing your flexibility of speech. Rather, make a short, bullet-pointed list with general ideas you want to address.

Although we don't typically realize it, we often rely on visual cues to understand the actual words a speaker is producing. Without these visual cues, some letters and sounds are easily interchangeable: for example "s" and "f," "m" and "n," and "p" and "b." This can be particularly problematic when providing a name, address, or e-mail address. To help avoid confusion, give example words for these types of letters. For example: "The e-mail address is jaynelatz@gmail.com. That's J as in Jack, A as in Apple, Y as in Yellow, N as in Nancy, E as in Edward, L as in Larry, A as in Apple, T as in Thomas, and Z as in Zebra at gmail dot com." Be mindful that this issue may also play a part when you are the listener. When taking down information such as an e-mail address, always repeat the information to your listener, using the above technique to help clarify problem letters.

Another major issue with telephone communication is the inability to visually gauge how your listener is reacting to your speech. This means you must carefully monitor your listener's verbal reactions and be alert for clues that they are not

fully understanding your message. If they are
uncharacteristically silent or don't seem to be
reacting as you would expect them to, they may
be having trouble understanding what it is you're
saying. In order to avoid this issue, frequently check
in with your listener verbally, periodically asking
them if they have any questions.

## Leaving the Perfect Voicemail

In today's hectic business world, it is becoming
more and more common for people to allow
their voicemail to act as their personal secretary,
screening their incoming calls and returning only
those they feel are a priority for them. This means
that learning to create a strong, effective voicemail
is an increasingly vital step in making day-to-day
professional connections.

The two key words that describe an effective
voicemail are "succinct" and "specific". Most people
view sifting through voicemails as a chore to be
accomplished as quickly as possible. Therefore,
voicemails that drag on for several minutes are
especially irritating and will negatively color the
recipient's view of the caller. If at all possible, keep
your message under thirty seconds. This timeframe
may seem short, but if you craft your message well, it
is more than enough. Before you pick up the phone,
think through what you want to say and decide what

the most important points are. This will help prevent you from rambling through a message, as well as help to eliminate unnecessary, unprofessional fillers such as "um" and "uh."

## The Four Parts of an Effective Voicemail

A good professional voicemail consists of only four parts: an introduction, your reason for calling, how you expect the listener to respond, and your contact information.

When introducing yourself, state your name and, if you do not contact this individual often, your company (e.g. "Hi, this is Jayne Latz with Corporate Speech Solutions."). If it is your first time calling, it may also help to establish a personal connection by identifying the individual who put you in contact.

When stating your reason for calling and how you expect the listener to respond, be as specific as possible. Do you want the listener to call you immediately? Is it acceptable if they respond via e-mail? If your listener knows exactly what is expected of them in their response and what the conversation will consist of, they are much more likely to return your call.

Finally, when leaving your contact information, speak as slowly and clearly as possible. There are few things more irritating than having to listen and re-listen to a message because the caller spoke too quickly and you missed part of their message. In many cases, these voicemails are deleted outright. Take a deep breath before speaking, clearly enunciate each word, and speak more slowly than you normally would in a typical phone conversation. One trick for ensuring that your contact information is received is to state your phone number at the introduction of your voicemail along with your greeting (e.g., "Hi, this is Jayne Latz with Corporate Speech Solutions at 212.308.7725."). This way, if the other party does need to replay your message, they only need to listen to the initial portion rather than sitting through the entire message a second time. Be sure to put the pauses in to give them time to write down the number.

## Crafting a Polished Voicemail Greeting

If you're like most professionals, you're often far too busy to answer your phone, and you allow most calls to go through to voicemail. This means that for many colleagues, clients, and potential business connections, your voicemail greeting may be your first impression. Use the following ideas to help create a voicemail greeting that is professional, polished, and efficient.

**Keep it short:** The ideal voicemail greeting should be no longer than twenty to twenty-five seconds. This is especially important in light of the fact you will most likely have many repeat callers who would prefer not to listen to a lengthy greeting each time they call.

**Eliminate background noise:** While you may not notice the noise around you at your workspace, background noise like ringing phones, chatting coworkers, or a noisy heating system will be very noticeable to your caller. In addition to sounding unprofessional, this background noise can make your greeting difficult to understand. Find a quiet location before recording your greeting. Take a deep breath to add power to your voice before beginning the recording.

**Practice:** In order to create the smoothest greeting possible, write down what you want to say in advance. Then read it aloud several times before recording, so that you can say the entire greeting without stumbling or taking unnatural pauses.

**Content:** Your voicemail greeting should contain the following elements: A greeting including your name, company and position; a brief statement that you are unable to answer the phone at the moment; a request for the caller to leave a message; and if possible, a way to receive immediate assistance if needed (e.g., a secretary, receptionist, or alternate department).

**Slow and clear:** Most important, take care to speak even more slowly and clearly than usual. It doesn't matter how well your greeting is crafted if no one can understand it.

## Tricky Professional Situations

Communicating in the business world requires a certain level of finesse and skill. However, some situations are trickier than others. This section will guide you through strategies to navigate those situations in the business world that have the potential to become uncomfortable if handled incorrectly.

### Handling Conflict

In a perfect world, all our interactions with colleagues would be nothing but pleasant. But, we are all human, so conflicts are bound to occur once in a while. While you may not be able to prevent conflict situations, you can control how you approach them. The way in which you communicate with others during tense or negative situations can make all the difference in how the conversation goes. Here are some strategies for keeping a negative situation from becoming a negative relationship.

**Avoid direct questions:** This tip doesn't mean you can't ask directly for information you need. It just means you need to lead into the question with some pleasantries. For example, an employee is late for a meeting (again) and you want to find out why. You approach the employee after the meeting and ask one of the two following questions:

"Why were you late this morning?"

"I noticed you came into the meeting late this morning. Did something happen?"

Although both questions aim at the same information, the first is much more likely to generate a negative, defensive response from the employee. Phrase the question in a more polite way, and you are much more likely to get an honest, positive response.

**Postpone if emotions are high:** When people are feeling emotional, their rational capabilities suffer. This often results in saying things in the heat of the moment that you regret later. While this can be problematic in any situation, in a business setting it can irreparably damage your professional relationships and your career. If you find that you are becoming increasingly upset during a conversation with a colleague, postpone the discussion until you have had time to cool down and consider the situation rationally. Simply tell the other person that you don't have the time to continue this conversation at the moment, but you would like to talk about it at a later time and try to come to a solution that's positive for everyone. Make sure to set an actual time to continue the conversation so it doesn't get postponed indefinitely, laying the foundation for negative feelings between you and your colleague.

**Use "I" statements:** When you find yourself in a conflict with a colleague, watch how you phrase your sentences. Focusing your message on what the other person has done wrong will put him on the defensive. Instead, focus on your reaction. This is easier than it sounds: each time you find yourself about to start a statement with "you," take a second to rephrase and begin with "I." For example, rather than saying, "You clearly didn't prepare for the presentation. Your performance was extremely disappointing," you might say, "I was somewhat disappointed in your presentation today. I usually see a much higher caliber of work in your performance."

**Lead with a compliment:** This tactic is useful when you need to offer criticism, but don't want it to create a negative relationship. When voicing your displeasure, preface the criticism with a compliment to help keep the situation positive. For example, if you have an employee who is spending too much time socializing at work, you may approach the situation with the following: "I really appreciate the way you get along so well with your colleagues, and I like that you take the time to get to know them. However, I'm concerned that the time you spend conversing at the water cooler is affecting your productivity."

**Hold your tongue:** When someone has upset you, it's natural to want to address the situation immediately. While you certainly don't want to bottle up negative feelings and allow them to fester, taking some time to think through the situation can help avoid ugly confrontations. Take one or two minutes to think about what you want to say to the other person and more importantly, what exactly you hope to accomplish. Focus on this objective rather than your immediate feelings and you stand a much greater chance of solving the issue at hand and avoiding an unpleasant conflict.

**Take a different point of view:** There are two sides to every situation. The person you want to confront likely has a different take on the matter and possibly feels that you're at fault as well. Take some time to honestly examine things from the other party's viewpoint. Better yet, ask this person what his or her take on the situation is, and listen with an open mind. By taking the other person's point of view into consideration, you may be able to turn a potential conflict into an open dialogue.

## Gossip
Everyone wants to build rapport with their coworkers. Having a close relationship with the people you work with can make your place of business a more comfortable, pleasant place to

spend your Monday through Friday. Unfortunately, a common way for people to try to build this rapport is through gossip.

In general, talking about those around you can be a quick and easy way to form a bond. However, this type of bond tends to be superficial and fleeting. Gossiping breeds distrust; it's natural to wonder if this person is willing to talk about others with you, what might she say about you to others when you're not around?

While gossip can be dangerous anywhere, it's especially toxic in the workplace. A professional setting is where maintaining an honest and confident image is the most essential. By indulging in gossip with others in the workplace, you send the message that you are insecure and more interested in discussing what's happening in the lives of others than your professional performance. If you find yourself in a conversation with a coworker who tries to drag you into a gossip-laden conversation, simply find a reason to politely excuse yourself from the conversation and end the interaction. By doing this repeatedly, you send the message that you are uninterested in spreading gossip, and others will eventually stop approaching you with this type of conversation.

## Miscommunication

No matter how hard you work to hone your professional communication skills, communicating with others is never foolproof. Two people participating in the same conversation may walk away with entirely different ideas of what was actually said. How can you avoid misunderstandings and miscommunications?

**Rephrase and repeat:** After your conversation partner makes an important point, rephrase what was said and repeat it back to make sure you fully understand. For example, you might say, "So you're saying that you think outsourcing our production is the best course of action?" or "Just to make sure I understand you correctly, you need a minimum of three days to finish this project?"

**Ask questions:** If you have any uncertainty about what your conversation partner has said, don't be afraid to ask for clarification or more detail. For example, you may say, "You said that you weren't entirely happy with the way the research and development team has handled this project. Could you tell me a little more about what you mean by that?"

**Be direct:** People don't always say exactly what they mean, particularly in business communication. Trying to say something delicately or in the most pleasant way possible is certainly understandable, but you must make sure you still convey all of the essential information in a clear, direct manner. Often your conversation partner will not be as adept as you think at reading between the lines, and indirect speech may leave you both with different ideas about what was said.

## Saying No

There are definite advantages to being agreeable in the workplace. Saying yes to people can help you to create professional relationships and develop a strong rapport with your colleagues. However, there are definitely situations in which saying no can be beneficial, be it rejecting an idea you see as badly planned, or turning down a project you don't have the time for. But saying no doesn't have to put a strain on your relationships. Use the following techniques to help you say no with professionalism and grace.

**Lead them to your side:** Rather than simply rejecting an idea outright, think about what you feel is wrong with it. Then, instead of just stating those issues outright, ask questions that will lead the other person to see your point of view. By asking a few pointed questions, you can discreetly lead someone to see things from your angle, and avoid having to say no directly.

**Buy some time:** Sometimes saying no is appropriate, but the time and place isn't; for example, if the conversation is taking place in front of people with whom your conversation partner wouldn't want to lose face. When this is the case, instead of saying no immediately, tell your conversation partner you'd like to think about it, and then make an appointment to talk at a later time and express your opinion then.

**Try a different medium:** In some cases, in-person communication isn't the best way to say no to someone. For example, by deferring your response and replying by e-mail, you allow yourself to state your case and give the other person time to consider your response with less pressure than would exist if you were face-to-face. Carefully consider your situation and decide what type of communication is best for the circumstances.

## Negotiating a Raise

As a conscientious employee, you continually seek to develop and grow your professional skills and knowledge throughout your career. For this reason, you may find yourself in a position where you feel your current skill level is no longer being matched by your salary. Negotiating a raise can be a tricky topic, and many professionals avoid it for fear of sounding demanding or creating an uncomfortable situation. Use the following strategies to get the salary you deserve without damaging your professional relationships.

**Do your research:** The very first thing you should do before asking for a raise is gather information. Start by researching the typical compensation for your type of position. Use the internet to gather a basic salary range as well as an expected salary path (e.g., how the compensation may increase with experience or knowledge). Take into consideration variations that may result from your industry or particular company. Knowing whether your salary is above, below, or spot on for your position can help inform how you approach the conversation. You may also want to investigate the duties that are typically included in job descriptions for your type of position. If you find that you are doing more than is generally expected, you may want to use this to support your request.

Why should you get a raise? In justifying a higher salary, one rule of thumb is to focus only on your worth, never your need. Don't sit there and entertain your boss with tales of financial woe. Little Bobby's new braces and your ever-increasing rent are not your boss's problem. Remember, you are not paid based on your financial situation, but your value to the company. Focus on what you do for the company, and why you do it exceptionally well.

Have a mental list of your boss's expectations of your role in the company at the ready, so that you can demonstrate that you've not only met, but exceeded, them. The best way to do this is to give evidence. Come to the conversation prepared with numbers and specific examples that objectively demonstrate your high performance. A statement like "Under my management, sales have increased more than 15 percent per quarter for the past two years," is much harder to refute than "I am an excellent manager."

**Communicate with clarity and confidence:** It's not only important to consider what you want to say, but how to say it. Maintaining an air of confidence can be more convincing than your actual argument. As you make your case, speak at an even, relaxed pace—rushing your words will not only make it difficult for you to be understood, but you will come across as nervous and unsure of yourself. Likewise, make sure that you monitor your volume. A strong volume will provide an air of confidence and professionalism, but speaking too loudly will come across as aggressive. Finally, make sure that you are speaking as clearly as possible. Articulate each and every sound, and don't run your words together. This will allow you to appear more educated and competent, and will also ensure that your boss understands every word you are saying.

**Avoid comparisons:** Never compare yourself to another employee when discussing a raise. Any hint of "But so-and-so has only been with the company X number of years…" or "My productivity is twice that of so-and-so…" reeks of childish squabbling and entitlement. Rather than comparing or speaking disparagingly about a coworker, focus on what you have done to merit a salary increase.

**Use collaborative language:** Using "we" rather than "I" helps keep the tone positive and collaborative rather than demanding. Phrases like "Help me understand…" or "What could we do…" can also be great for setting a cooperative tone.

**Think ahead:** If you're turned down, don't simply end the conversation. Rather, set yourself up for a future conversation that's more likely to have a positive outcome. Ask your boss what specifically you can do to earn a raise in the coming year. Discuss goals and possible additional responsibilities. Also, be sure to set a benchmark for when you can expect to revisit the conversation, so that you know you and your boss are on the same page.

# CHAPTER 6

# The Fourth Step: Winning that Job or Promotion

The average American will hold between five and fifteen jobs over the course of his or her professional life. While these jobs may span several occupations or job descriptions, they will all hold one aspect in common: the interview process. This chapter focuses on guiding you through the necessary steps of landing the job, from crafting a polished cover letter and résumé through negotiating terms of employment.

## Acing the Interview

Communication is an essential skill in almost any job, and a key skill most employers look for during an interview. Speaking with clarity and confidence and demonstrating a dynamic speaking voice can go a long way toward making a positive impression. What else can you do that will help you ace the interview and land your dream job?

## Building Rapport

While interviewers are certainly interested in your qualifications and experience, a less concrete factor that gives one candidate an edge over another is how the interviewer feels during the interview. This may not make its way into the official notes, but if an interviewer feels pleasant and at ease during the interview, he will subconsciously associate these feelings with you. In order to make the interview as pleasant as possible, use the following techniques:

**Smile:** Often people maintain a serious disposition during interviews, believing that this gives them an air of professionalism. However, being overly serious can create a sense of discomfort and make you appear unpleasant. Smiling, on the other hand, makes you seem approachable and friendly, characteristics that everyone wants in a coworker or employee. This simple facial expression can make a world of difference in how others feel around you.

**Use the interviewer's name:** Hearing one's own name out loud creates a positive feeling and makes the listener subconsciously feel more connected to the speaker. Aim to use the interviewer's name two to three times over the course of the interview.

**Relax:** Of course, it is difficult to relax when having a conversation that may determine your professional future. However, if you are obviously nervous and uncomfortable, it will make your interviewer uncomfortable as well. While you certainly don't want to come across as overly casual, you do want to relax enough to allow your personality to shine through.

**Be enthusiastic and positive:** Discuss your past and future in a positive tone. Avoid speaking negatively about past jobs, bosses, or colleagues. Potential employers subconsciously envision themselves in the position of your past employers. Therefore, a negative comment about a former boss or company may create an unpleasant reaction.

## The Day of the Interview

Whether or not an interview leads to your dream job is more than just luck; interviewing well is a skill you can learn and practice in advance to increase your chances of landing that dream job. What can you do to ensure that you perform your best the day of the interview?

**Punctuality:** Don't just be on time—try to arrive at your destination approximately fifteen minutes before your scheduled interview. This will give you time to collect yourself and mentally prepare. If you are unfamiliar with the location, take a dry run to the interview site a day or two in advance to make sure you don't find yourself driving in circles on the big day.

**Turn your cell phone off:** Don't just silence your phone—make sure it is actually off during the interview. A buzzing, vibrating device in your pocket or purse can be just as distracting as a loud ring.

**Have your résumé in hand:** While your interviewer will most likely bring your résumé to the interview, you should always have a copy on hand as well, just in case. Your interviewer is probably very busy and seeing many people for the position. Being prepared in case she isn't will help you to appear responsible and organized.

**Handshake:** As was previously discussed, handshakes are crucial. The way you shake hands may be one of your interviewer's first impressions of you. As you shake your interviewer's hand, look him in the eye and smile. Give firm pressure, but don't squeeze—you want to convey strength and confidence, but you don't want to hurt him. Duration is also important. Don't pull your hand away too soon; pay attention to your interviewer's hand and follow his lead.

## Responding to Questions

While you may not have control over which questions your interviewer chooses to ask, you can control your responses. The way in which you respond can be as important as the content itself. At my company, we provide training for clients in a variety of professional fields to help them prepare for, and ace, interviews. One very important activity is working on unexpected questions and answers.

**Length is key:** When responding, be aware of the length of your answers. While you don't want to rush and need to make sure you answer the question in full, you should also be on guard against lengthy, rambling answers. Many interviewees find themselves babbling on and on when they get nervous, and often end up quite off topic by the end of their response. Make sure that each of your answers fits the exact question asked.

**Clear and slow:** Remember to use good speech skills in your answers. Put extra effort into good pronunciation and clear speech, and maintain a slow, steady pace. If your interviewer can't understand your responses, you may lose the job right then and there.

**Content:** Be specific and give strong examples when responding to the interviewer's questions, especially when discussing your strengths or personal job history. Anyone can say they are good at their job, but giving a personal example (e.g., sales rose 43 percent during your time at your last company) makes your answer much stronger. Whenever possible, try to tailor these examples to the specific needs of the company you are interviewing for.

**Follow up:** A day or two after your interview, follow up with a well-written note to your interviewer thanking him for his time and consideration. Be sure to proofread the note before sending. Not only is this professional and considerate, it helps to keep your name fresh in the mind of the interviewer.

## What Not to Do

There are some communication issues that can derail even the strongest of interviews. All of the concepts in Chapter 3 should be applied during your interview to ensure that you come across as a strong, professional communicator. In particular, be aware of:

**Tone issues:** A common speech issue is raising the tone of one's voice at the end of a sentence so that a statement sounds like a question. This habit is fairly common and acceptable in casual conversation between friends. However, in a professional situation, it can make you sound unsure of yourself.

**Mumbling:** Make sure that your speech is crisp and clear. Mumbling can make you sound lazy and overly relaxed. While you want to remain natural, make sure that you are pronouncing all of the letters and sounds of each word.

**Avoid filler words:** Using words like "um" and "like" will detract from your message and make you sound sloppy. Take a moment and pause if you need it, but don't add in unnecessary words to fill the silence.

**Project your voice:** Often people speak too quietly and hesitantly in the presence of authority figures. While you may think this sounds polite and deferent, it actually can make you appear unsure of yourself and shy. Project your voice with a strong clear tone to appear more professional and confident.

**Steer clear of slang:** The language you use in a casual conversation is not the same language you should use in a professional situation. This can be particularly tricky for young job candidates new to the interview process. Many phrases and words, which seem natural to you, may be completely inappropriate to the workplace. Take some time to assess your language and figure out which slang words or phrases you use most often. Then challenge yourself to go a full day without using them. You can even enlist a friend or two to help by having them point out each time you accidentally use the slang.

**Don't rush:** Often people rush their speech when nervous (and who isn't nervous during a job interview?). Slow down to appear more competent and thoughtful. Take a pause in your speech every now and then to take a breath and allow your interviewer to absorb your message.

# SECTION III

## What's Next?

# CHAPTER 7

# How to Rise to the Top of the Ladder

So far we've covered strategies for specific aspects of communication, from ways to improve your speech to difficult social situations particular to a professional environment. In this chapter we conclude with some general reminders for good communication skills applicable to the workplace as well as your day-to-day communication.

## E-Mail Communication

Even though e-mail has become the most widely used form of business communication, many people still use inappropriate e-mail practices, making their communication seem unprofessional and sloppy. Use the following techniques to create the most effective business e-mail you can:

### Etiquette
**Use the subject line properly:** Avoid using a generic

subject such as "Hello" or "Information" or, even worse, leaving it blank altogether. Using a specific and meaningful subject will help both you and the recipient better categorize and organize the e-mail.

**Don't neglect the greeting:** Always begin with a greeting such as To Whom It May Concern or Dear Mr. Smith. Jumping into your message without a formal greeting may come across as aggressive or overly casual.

**Use proper writing:** Always use proper grammar and punctuation. Remember that e-mail is simply an electronic form of a letter. You would never neglect proper grammar or punctuation in a business letter, yet people often feel it is okay when writing e-mail. Always run a spell check and double check your writing. For very important e-mails, print a copy and read it over on paper. For most people, it is easier to catch a mistake on paper than it is on a computer screen.

**Avoid electronic faux pas:** Never write using all capital letters. USING ALL CAPS IS THE ELECTRONIC VERSION OF SHOUTING. You should also avoid the conventions of texting (e.g., "lol" "brb" or "ttyl") as well as emoticons. While these can add a personal touch in texting, they have no place in business e-mail.

## Privacy

E-mail has certainly made business communication more efficient. Unfortunately, it also comes with a host of new privacy issues, which were not a concern with traditional mail. Take the following into consideration in your professional e-mail communication to protect your privacy and that of others:

**The "To" field:**  Double check to whom you're sending your e-mail before pressing "Send." One drawback of e-mail is how easy it can be to send a message to an unintended recipient. Many e-mail services automatically fill in the "To" field on e-mail with suggestions from your contact list after only a few letters have been typed. This may be convenient, but makes sending e-mail to the wrong recipient very easy. Another dangerous situation is group e-mails. When replying to group e-mail, only select the "Reply All" option if you are positive the e-mail is relevant and appropriate for everyone on the list.

**Sensitive information:** Even if you're careful about who you're sending your e-mail to, it is still not as secure as you might think. Unless you take additional steps, e-mail is not encrypted, which means that it is possible for someone to intercept and read it once it's on its way to its intended recipient. Because of this possibility, you should never send sensitive information over e-mail, especially credit card numbers or other financial information or usernames and passwords.

You should also avoid sending information that could be potentially damaging to you or someone else's career or personal reputation. Even if the e-mail is sent in a completely secure manner, once the e-mail is in the recipient's hands, it is out of your control. The information could then be transmitted to someone else, either accidentally or on purpose.

## General Etiquette

In the business world, we're often so concerned with speaking professionally and selling the finer points of our expertise that we forget one of the most fundamental necessities of making connections with others: etiquette. The following are aspects of common courtesy that are basic, but all too often, left by the wayside in professional interaction.

**Don't ignore your voicemail:** In today's interconnected society it's easy to become overwhelmed with the number of messages flooding our smartphones and inboxes. However, despite this flood of contact, it's imperative to return each message in a timely manner. Leaving a message and then waiting days to receive a reply is incredibly frustrating and creates the sense that the other person is rude and has no consideration for you or your time. In order to help organize your time, set aside a specific time during each workday in which you only reply to voicemail, e-mail, and other correspondence. If you find this is still somewhat daunting, break the task into two time periods: one to tackle messages from the morning, and one for messages received during the latter half of the day.

**Greetings count:** When someone enters the room and greets you, it is generally appropriate to stand up and shake their hand. By formally acknowledging their entrance, you send the message that you consider them and their reason for speaking to you a priority. Even if the situation is slightly less formal, or concerns a person you see regularly, this extra gesture adds a touch of professionalism and class to your interaction.

**Silence please:** Although our phones are now able to keep us in constant contact with those around us, the incessant buzzing and beeping that comes from all of those e-mails, texts, calls, and voicemails can be incredibly distracting. Whenever possible, keep your phone on vibrate, and never check incoming messages in the middle of a professional interaction. In a meeting or other formal situation, don't just put your phone on vibrate; silence it or turn it off altogether. In a quiet room, even the buzz of a vibrating phone can be distracting.

**Introductions:** When introducing two people, it's customary to introduce the younger or lower-ranking person to the higher-ranking person, such as a boss, client, or distinguished guest. The best way to remember this is the higher-ranking person's name comes first. For example, if your boss is Mrs. Brown, you might say, "Mrs. Brown, I'd like you to meet my new administrative assistant, Sarah." However, the most important thing about introductions is that they happen; failing to introduce two people at the appropriate time can create an uncomfortable situation. If you are having trouble recalling someone's name, simply admit it casually by saying something like, "I'm sorry, your name has slipped my mind at the moment." If you are unsure of whether two people have been introduced or not, err on the side of caution and ask, "Have you two met?"

**Don't ignore the basics:** As our society becomes more hectic and rushed, the most basic aspects of courtesy and manners often fall by the wayside. "Please" and "Thank you" remain two of the most important phrases in the English language—use them often.

**Admit your mistakes (gracefully):** No matter how smooth your etiquette is, everyone has a lapse in manners once in a while. Should this happen to you, acknowledge your mistake and apologize. Be sincere in your apology, but don't go overboard; if you make a big issue of the matter, it will only serve to make the other person uncomfortable and draw more attention to your mistake.

## Empathy

When communicating in the professional world, one of the most important keys to successful interaction is to understand the other person's point of view. Whether you are speaking with a client, colleague, or your boss, understanding where your communication partner is coming from will help you to create strong, successful communication.

One of the most essential skills to better understand another person's perspective is to comprehend what he wants. Try to consider what best serves the other person's needs and then frame your conversation and interaction based on that. If a person feels that the topic at hand is aimed at his best interest, he will be much more receptive.

However, in order to truly be empathetic to another's point of view, you need to not only understand what he wants, but why it is important and valid. This higher level of more sincere understanding not only helps to foster strong communicative interactions, but also helps to develop stronger business relationships as a whole by establishing trust and promoting collaboration. To this end, ask your communication partner questions and truly listen to the answers. Before an important conversation, it may also help to do some research into the background of the other person's company or situation, especially if he is unfamiliar or a recent acquaintance.

## Face-to-face Time

Thanks to technology, it is easier than ever to stay in near constant contact with our colleagues, clients, and customers. Between smartphones, laptops, tablets, and voicemail, business communication is typically only the touch of a button away. While this can be convenient, it has led to a sharp decrease in the amount of time we spend in face-to-face contact. While some consider this a timesaver, there are drawbacks to this lack of in-person communication. Why is face-to-face communication so important?

- Talking with someone in person helps you to establish a personal connection. Establishing a relationship in this way can lead to more positive results, not only in the short term, but in future interactions as well.

- Even though technology seems to be more efficient, face-to-face communication can actually save you time. All too often we end up playing phone tag or participating in never-ending e-mail discussions attempting to settle a point or answer a question. In face-to-face discussions, you can ask questions on the spot and avoid the days-long volleying that often accompanies other types of communication.

- Nonverbal cues can make communication richer and more effective. You can often learn more about your conversation partner via facial expression, tone, and body posture than his words alone. Without these nonverbal cues, it's very easy to misunderstand or misinterpret the intention of written communication. This makes face-to-face communication especially important when dealing with delicate matters or important professional interactions.

Although an in-person visit isn't always feasible, in general the more personal the contact the better. This means that, typically, e-mail is better than a text, a phone call is better than e-mail, and an in-person visit is better than a phone call. If an in-person visit is not feasible, then a virtual face-to-face meeting would be the next ideal option. If the discussion would benefit from give and take, then face-to-face communication is definitely your best course of action. However, for a brief, concrete matter, like confirming a meeting time, e-mail is usually preferable.

Even though the chaos of our professional lives may make texting or e-mail seem like the best option, it is worth taking the time to communicate on a more personal level to help ensure clearer, more effective communication.

## Misused Words

Everyone wants to sound as professional as possible when communicating in a business setting. Working on clear, understandable speech is important, but it is only one piece of the puzzle. Often people include inaccuracies in their speech that they are completely unaware of. The following are some very commonly misused words that you may be unaware of:

*"The news was so shocking, my jaw was **literally** in my lap."*

The word *literally* refers to the reality of an event. Unless the speaker's jaw was actually touching his knees, this is an inaccurate use of the word literally. The speaker actually means that it occurred *figuratively*—he is using the phrase as a metaphor to exaggerate or emphasize the point. For proper usage, simply omit the word *literally* and keep the sentence as it is. The metaphor will speak for itself.

*"He continued to work **irregardless** of his exhaustion."*

*Irregardless* is not a word. It is an erroneous combination of two separate words: regardless and *irrespective*. Both words mean "in spite of." Any usage of this word is wrong. Period.

*"I like to **peruse** the paper for a few minutes as I drink my coffee each morning."*

People often use *peruse* to mean to glance over something or to read or review it quickly and superficially. However, the word actually means the near opposite of that: to read with thoroughness or care.

## Difficult Definitions

The following are words that many people misunderstand the definitions of. Using one in the incorrect manner can not only be confusing to the listener, but can make it seem that you are attempting to use larger vocabulary words to sound more intelligent without fully understanding them. These are only a very small sampling of words that are often misunderstood and misused. As a general rule, only use a vocabulary word if you are 100 percent sure that you know its definition and are using it correctly.

## nonplussed

*Incorrect definition:* calm, not worried

"She had prepared so thoroughly for her presentation that she was completely nonplussed when the CEO asked if he could watch."

*Correct definition:* perplexed, confused

"The secretary's handwriting was so messy, he simply stared at the memo nonplussed, unable to understand a word of it."

## bemused

*Incorrect definition:* amused
"Rob was bemused at the comical story."

*Correct definition:* confused (similar to nonplussed)
"My boss was bemused by the overly complicated minutes of the meeting."

## enormity

*Incorrect definition: the quality of being very large*
"They were awed by the enormity of the canyon."

*Correct definition:* the quality of being monstrous or very immoral
"The enormity of the crimes committed during the war was truly disturbing."

## Written Mistakes

People often incorrectly interchange the following words in their writing. Use the following rules as a guide to make sure your usage is correct:

**they're / their / there:**

- "They're" is a combination of they and are, and is only used in situations in which those two words would be appropriate. For example, "They are from China," could be rewritten as "They're from China."

- "Their" is a possessive pronoun used to demonstrate ownership. For example, the sentence "Mary and Jim's daughter is three years old," may be rewritten as, "Their daughter is three years old."

- "There" demonstrates location. For example, "The bottle is way over there."

**your / you're:**

- "Your," like "their," is a possessive pronoun, and is used to demonstrate ownership. For example, "Your shoes are in the kitchen."

- "You're" is a contraction of the two words "you" and "are." For example, "You're a wonderful boss."

**affect / effect:**

> "Affect" is a verb and "effect" is a noun. A good
> way to remember this is a verb is an action
> word, and both "action" and "affect" start
> with *a*. The following sentences are examples
> of correct usage:
>
> > "The pills can *affect* your mood."
> >
> > "The pills can cause strange side *effects*."

## Avoiding Pretension

Even if you are completely sure of a vocabulary
word's meaning, make sure that it is appropriate
for use in the given situation. Often people make
the mistake of equating an impressive vocabulary
with being articulate. While this is true to an
extent, using uncommon language that few people
understand doesn't make you seem particularly
intelligent. Unfortunately, it often just makes your
message difficult to understand.

This mistake is commonly found with non-native
speakers of a language, particularly in writing.
Unsure of their grammatical or linguistic skills,
many attempt to overcompensate with unnecessarily
difficult words, hoping it will give the impression
that they are educated and knowledgeable. However,
when language is difficult to understand, many
people will tune out and your message will be lost.

In addition, constantly using what you consider to be impressive vocabulary can make you appear unapproachable or snobbish. While you certainly want to maintain professional language and avoid slang, overly lengthy or obscure words will ultimately hurt your message.

When in doubt, refer to the old saying: KISS (Keep It Short and Simple).

## Listening Skills

Never forget: Communication is a two-way street. It doesn't matter how phenomenal you are at speaking—if your listening skills are lacking, your communication will still suffer. Recently a CEO of a company complained to me that an employee that he was referring to me for training "just doesn't listen. For instance, when someone poses a question to him he appears to ignore the question and answers with a completely extraneous remark."

Use the following suggestions to ensure your listening skills are up to par.

**Listen actively:** Don't just passively absorb what your conversational partner is saying. Ask questions, make comments, and otherwise encourage your speaker. If you find a point especially interesting, ask the speaker to elaborate or to give details and examples. If something is unclear, ask for clarification. Or if you are unsure you are getting the point, rephrase what the person has just said to make sure you understand. For example, you might say, "If I understand correctly, you're saying that_____. Is that right?" This helps ensure that you receive the message and also signals to the speaker that you are invested in the conversation.

**Silence is golden:** Don't interrupt your partner. Often people are so eager to demonstrate their knowledge or to give input, they cut off their speaker or try to finish her sentences. Avoid this at all costs. It will do nothing but offend your conversational partner and make you appear rude. Instead, not only wait until your partner has finished speaking, but allow a pause before you respond. This focuses your listener's attention and also gives the impression that you put value into her message.

**Read between the lines:** Often a speaker may not say exactly what it is she's thinking or feeling. Try to gather extra meaning from inferences and nonverbal cues, such as tone of voice or facial expression. You'll be surprised at how much extra information you can gather just by paying attention.

## Communicating with Non-native English Speakers

With globalization on the rise, the workplace is becoming an increasingly multicultural environment. Chances are, nearly everyone reading this book has at least one colleague, customer, or work-related acquaintance who is a non-native speaker of English. When communicating with non-native speakers of English, many people try to compensate in ways that are not helpful to their listeners—for example, speaking more loudly. These misguided attempts at enhancing communication often do nothing but make your listeners uncomfortable. There are, however, simple ways to make you more easily understood when speaking with people whose first language is not English:

**Slow down:** It often takes more time for a non-native speaker to process the words that are being spoken. Since missing one or two words can confuse the entire message, this is a significant problem. Slowing down your rate to a more leisurely and more professional pace will give your listener time to process and understand each word of your message.

**Speak clearly:** Native speakers of a language will generally run their words together in conversational speech, so that the end of one word blends with the beginning of the next. This can cause difficulty for a person who has learned to hear and understand words in isolation. If your listener seems not to understand, clearly separate the words of the phrase or sentence that is causing confusion.

**Use another word:** It doesn't matter how slowly and clearly you speak if your listener has never learned the words you are using. If your listener seems to be unfamiliar with a word, try to use a simpler word that has the same meaning.

**Avoid slang and idioms:** As native speakers of English, our daily communication is constantly laced with slang and idioms. Recently we had an international client ask her manager to retain our services specifically to improve her knowledge of idiomatic expressions. The term "layman" had been used in a meeting and she was concerned that she did not know the meaning. Think of all the terms and phrases we use which don't mean exactly what they say: "Drop me a line," "On the fence," "Seeing red"—the list goes on and on. If your listener looks confused, think about what you just said and use the most literal language possible.

**Rephrase:** Often it is not only the individual words, but the construction of the sentence itself which can be confusing. If your listener looks lost, try repeating your sentence in a different, simpler way. In extreme situations, using gestures may also be helpful.

## Multicultural Considerations in Communication

In addition to the somewhat obvious problem of language barriers, there are other significant differences in how people communicate in different cultures. Take the following aspects of communication into consideration when interacting with professionals from different backgrounds and cultures.

## Eye Contact

In American culture, eye contact is generally considered a positive thing. Maintaining strong eye contact with a conversation partner signifies self-confidence and an interest in what the other person in saying. In addition, a lack of eye contact is often read as a sign of dishonesty. It's common to hear an American express sentiments like, "There was something I didn't trust about him; he wouldn't look me in the eye."

While a lack of eye contact may indicate dishonesty to an American, it is often used as a sign of respect in other cultures, particularly those of East Asia. In some cultures, it is common etiquette to avert your eyes from an authority figure or professional superior. Therefore, an employee unfamiliar with American culture may spend much of a conversation with her boss gazing at the floor or the desk in front of her rather than looking at the boss directly in the eye. Differences in eye contact can also be found within the same culture, often among different religious or racial groups. For example, practitioners of some religions consider prolonged eye contact with a member of the opposite sex inappropriate. In addition, one study conducted found racial differences in how eye contact is utilized within American culture.

Because eye contact can be such a loaded form of nonverbal communication, it's important that you understand what it may mean to the person you are talking to. Although you cannot make assumptions based on an individual's cultural background, you can observe your conversation partner's behavior, and adjust your own behavior accordingly.

## Personal Space

The distance at which someone feels comfortable standing from another person is greatly influenced by their culture and the social situation. For example, the range of comfort for the average American is typically one-and-a-half to three feet away from another person. In business situations, Americans will tend toward the further end of this range (two to three feet). The distance shrinks with those whom the individual is most comfortable; with a romantic partner, family member or close friend, personal space is reduced greatly. On the other end of the spectrum, Americans tend to increase their comfort distance with strangers, positioning themselves as far as comfortably possible from a stranger they are not conversing with. Americans also tend to avoid touching others, especially in professional situations. Physical contact beyond a handshake is typically reserved for close friends and family.

People from Mediterranean, Hispanic, and Middle Eastern cultures will often have a much closer comfort distance than Americans. For many, a distance of less than one-and-a-half feet is perfectly acceptable and will convey a sense of personal connection. Therefore, an American who physically pulls back from a person from one of these cultures may appear aloof or unfriendly. These cultures are also much more likely to touch their conversation partner; a light touch on the arm to emphasize a point or a pat on the shoulder are perfectly acceptable and much more common than in typical American culture.

On the other end of the spectrum are those from East Asian cultures. Typically, the proximity from one's conversation partner is increased in these cultures and physical contact is rare in professional situations. In some Asian cultures, touching can even be considered disrespectful. For example, touching anyone, even children, on the head is viewed as quite offensive for some. In Middle Eastern cultures, touching is generally considered unacceptable between members of the opposite sex.

## Potential Cultural Faux Pas

In addition to basic aspects of communication, there are some specific situations that can cause misunderstandings between individuals from different cultural backgrounds. Take a look at the following to avoid offense and increase understanding:

**Business cards:** While Americans trade business cards with one another very casually, this practice is given a much higher level of respect in other cultures. For example, many East Asian cultures regard the business card as an extension of the individual's professional image, and treat the exchange of cards quite seriously. A card is always received with both hands and then read carefully before being put into the receiver's wallet. Writing on a business card in such a situation is considered extremely impolite. When receiving the business card of a professional from a culture you are unfamiliar with, err on the side of caution, and treat the card with respect.

**Gestures:** Gestures which may be completely inoffensive or even complimentary in one culture can be offensive in others. Take for example, former President Richard Nixon's visit to Brazil. When exiting his plane, he gave the okay sign as it is understood in America: index finger to thumb, all other fingers extended. Unfortunately for President Nixon, in Brazil (as well as Germany and Russia) this is an exceedingly vulgar sign. In other cultures, a thumbs-up gesture or V with the palm facing the body are considered insulting, somewhat analogous to the American version of the middle finger. As a precaution, avoid using hand signals or gestures that may be uniquely American when dealing with professionals from another country or culture.

**Greeting:** Before traveling to another country or conducting business with a company from another culture, be aware of the most common form of greeting. Some cultures greet one another with a slight bow at the waist with no physical contact, while in others a handshake combined with a kiss on the cheek is customary. With the rise of international business, many cultures now expect the Americanized handshake, so it is often a safe bet. However, some cultures and religions frown upon physical contact between opposite sexes; if you find yourself in a situation in which you proffer your hand and it is declined, politely accept, apologize, and move on.

**Smiling:** Although a smile may seem like the most straightforward of all types of communication, in reality smiling is used in different ways in different cultures. For example, in some East Asian cultures, people offer a smile when embarrassed or confused. In Japanese culture, a smile is often considered a sign of frivolity, so smiling is avoided in important situations, so as not to give the impression that the individual isn't taking the occasion seriously. When dealing with individuals from another culture, make sure you understand the possible reasons that they may or may not offer a smile in order to avoid misunderstandings and confusion. In addition, be aware that your friendly smile may hold more meaning for your conversation partner than you realize.

**Titles:** The way a person addresses colleagues can vary from culture to culture. As a general rule, never address someone by their first name until invited to do so—in some cultures this can be considered disrespectful. In other cultures, specific titles are used. In America, it is common to address someone as "Doctor Smith" or "Professor Jones," but our use of title typically stops there. In other countries, for instance, Mexico, titles are used more frequently and for a wider variety of positions, for example, Engineer, Architect, or even Licenciado (licensed one), a term used for anyone holding a college degree.

While being aware of a person's culture is a good starting point for how to conduct yourself in conversation, each person is different and may have different standards and expectations. Never assume a person will behave a certain way based on their culture alone. When in doubt, simply observe how your conversation partner conducts him- or herself and mirror that behavior.

# CHAPTER 8

# After the Climb

Your communication success does not end
when you get to the top. In many ways, it is just
beginning. Communication is the exchange and
flow of information from one person to another.
The process entails a sender transmitting the idea
to the receiver. Business leaders must possess
strong communication skills and exude confidence
whenever they are conveying ideas to their team.
Strong communication skills include everything
we discussed in this book from the actual vocal
production to the nonverbal messages we send daily.
A poor communicator is one where the receiver
fails to clearly understand the idea being conveyed.
There are many aspects of communication that
reflect your leadership skills. How you communicate
and share ideas will impact the effectiveness of
group communication within your business or
organization. Today's global marketplace places
greater demands on strong communication skills
than ever before.

In order to permanently improve your speech, it is essential to regularly practice what you learn. You will find with practice over time that you no longer have to concentrate on each of these techniques. The techniques will become routine like any other learned skill. In the same way that you don't consciously think about each move as you ride a bicycle, your new speech skills will become second nature and will require little to no conscious effort.

I look forward to hearing stories of your rise up the corporate ladder. Please reach out to me on LinkedIn, Facebook or Twitter (@jaynelatz) to share your success stories. You recall the examples of experiences by some of my clients in the past. Now I want to hear from you. In closing, using your communication skills to climb the ladder is an ongoing process. The tools in this book will not only help you to rise to the top but will help you surpass your professional dreams. I wish you all the best on your journey.

# About the Author

Jayne Latz is CEO of Corporate Speech Solutions, LLC (CSS), facilitating both individuals and groups in Fortune 500 companies and small businesses with proven strategies to accelerate communication effectiveness. CSS has guided employees and executives from PricewaterhouseCoopers, Ltd., Citigroup, and Harry Winston, to name a few. As a licensed speech-language pathologist, professional speaker, speech trainer, and coach with twenty-five plus years of experience, Latz launched CSS in 2006, customizing speech improvement and accent-reduction training programs to suit individuals and groups for both business and personal success. Latz taught at New York University for six years and mentored graduate students for twenty years. Her background provides her with the unique skill set to transform the corporate communication skills of both individuals and groups, with a goal that every participant develops the ability to communicate with clarity and confidence. Latz is a current member of the National Speakers Association, a featured speaker of the New York State Society for Certified Public Accountants, and is co-author of *Talking Business: When English is Your Second*

*Language.* She has been featured in *The Wall Street Journal,* on the "Today" show, and on air with NPR.

Made in the USA
Columbia, SC
11 March 2018